Design	David West
	Children's Book Design
Editor	Margaret Fagan
Editorial planning	Clark Robinson Limited
Researcher	Cecilia Weston-Baker
Illustrators	Alex Pang
	Galina Zolfaghari
Consultant	Alan Morton PhD
	Science Museum, London

© Aladdin Books 1989
Designed and produced by
Aladdin Books Ltd
70 Old Compton Street
London W1

First published in
Great Britain in 1989 by
Franklin Watts
12a Golden Square
London W1

ISBN 0 86313 933 7

Printed in Belgium

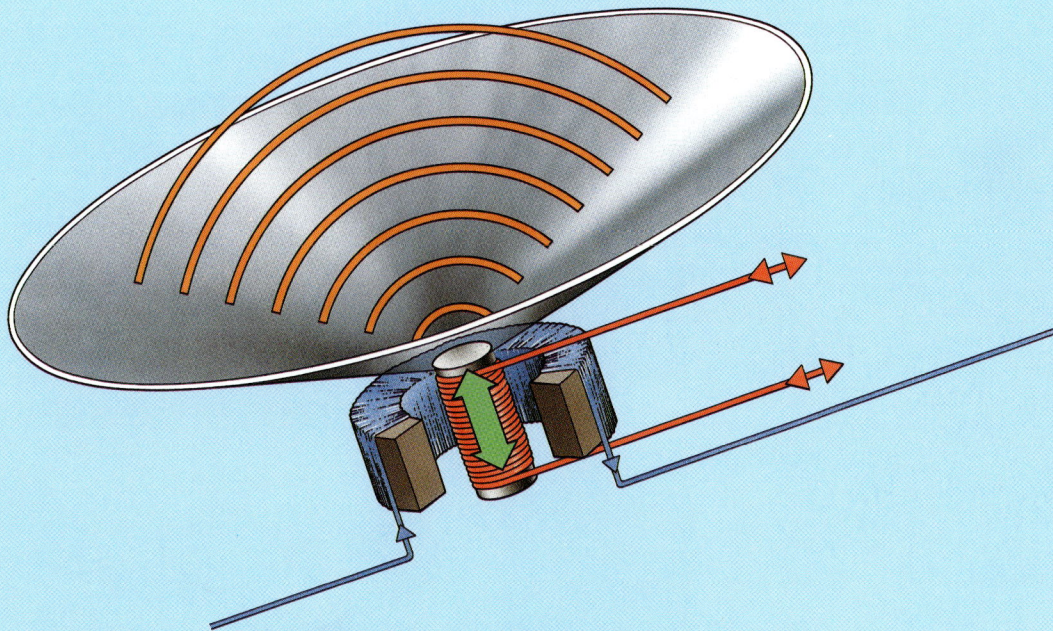

GLOUCESTER PRESS
London · New York · Toronto · Sydney

Contents

This book will tell you about magnetism — bar magnets to dynamos.
Every page is set out as shown below with an introduction to science ideas, and "hands on" projects for you to do with simple equipment. There are also quizzes and there is a section about important discoveries at the back of the book.

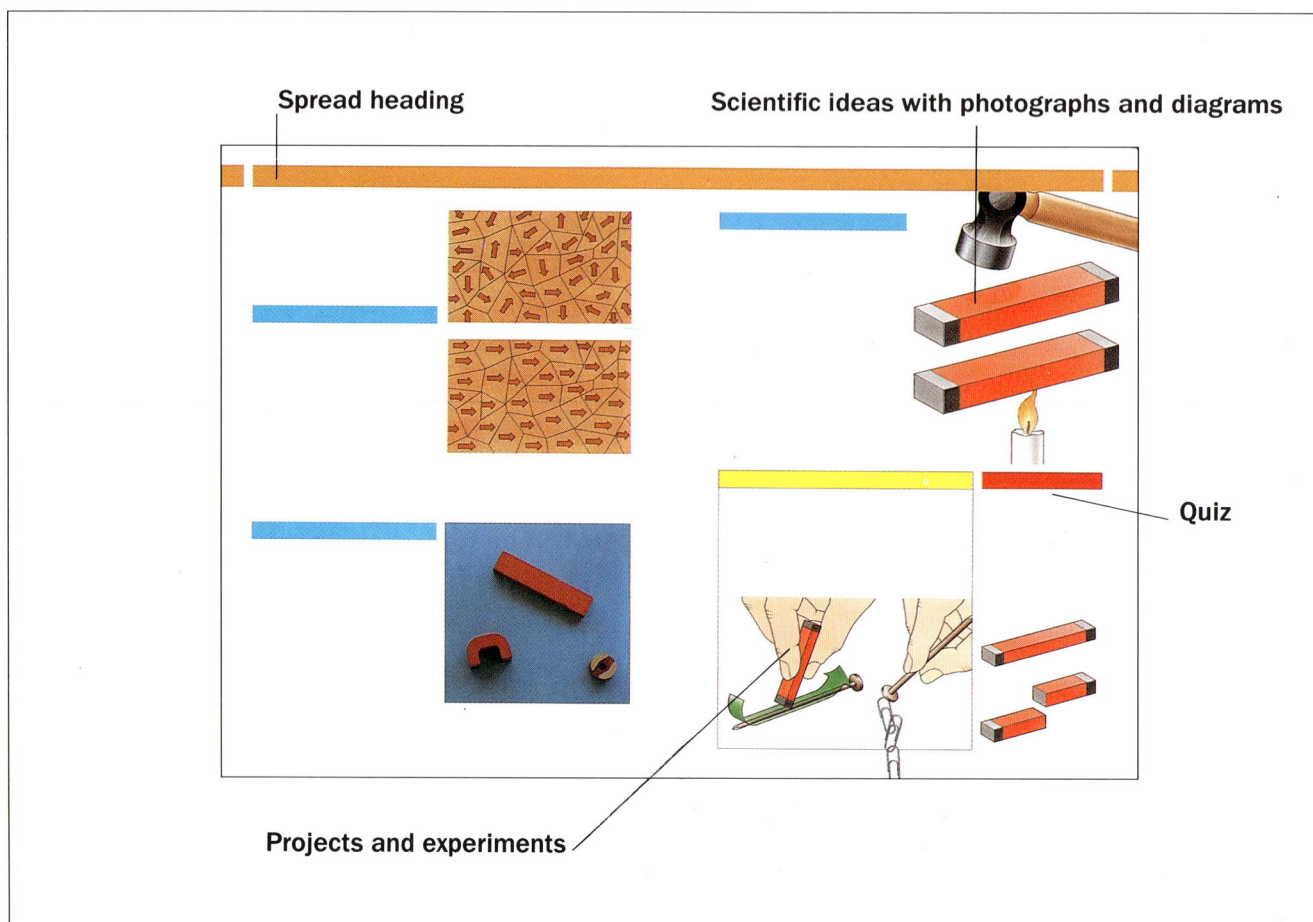

Spread heading

Scientific ideas with photographs and diagrams

Quiz

Projects and experiments

Introduction

There are two main types of magnets. A permanent magnet is made of a magnetic material such as iron or ferrite. It keeps its magnetism all the time. An electromagnet consists of a coil of wire. It becomes a magnet when an electric current is passed through the wire that makes up the coil. Some electromagnets have a piece of iron inside the coil to make the magnet stronger. Electromagnets are magnetic only when the electric current flows. As a result, they can be switched on and off.

Magnets have many uses, from keeping a refrigerator door shut to storing millions of numbers in a computer. They are key components of tape recorders, television sets, microphones and loudspeakers. Magnets in compasses enable ships and aircraft to find their way around the world. They are also used in various machines, such as dynamos and electric motors.

The strange effects of magnetism: a magnet floats above a superconducting metal

More than 2,000 years ago, the Greeks found a type of black stone with strange powers. Iron nails and pins clung to the stone. If a piece of the stone was hung from a string, it always pointed in the same direction. These black stones from Magnesia, (a place in modern day Turkey) were called magnets.

WHAT IS A MAGNET?

Some substances, such as magnetite, are natural magnets. A magnet can attract, or pull closer, small pieces of iron. The power of attracting pieces of iron in this way is called magnetism. Some magnets are called permanent magnets. They keep their magnetism, unless they are dropped, knocked or get too hot. Some materials can be made to act like magnets when an electric current is passed through them. They are called electromagnets. They are not permanent magnets, because their magnetism can be turned on and off with an electric current.

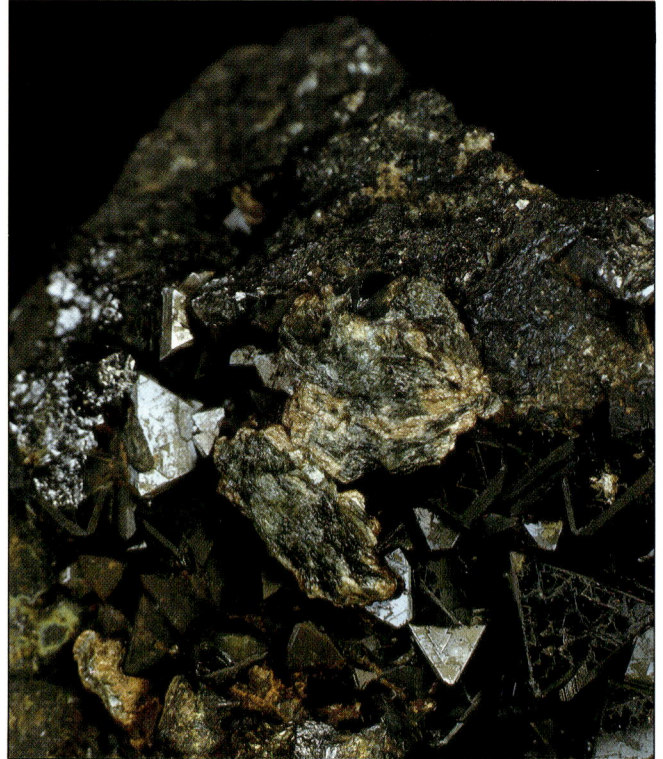

▲ Magnetite is also called lodestone, or "leading stone". In the ancient world, lodestones were used like compasses to guide travellers.

DIFFERENT KINDS OF MAGNETS

Most magnets are made from iron or steel, a metal made by adding carbon and other substances to iron. Magnets can also be made from more expensive metals, such as nickel and cobalt. Strong magnets are made by mixing aluminium, nickel, cobalt, iron and samarium.

Some magnets are long and narrow. They are called bar magnets. Other magnets are curved like horseshoes, and are called horseshoe magnets. Magnets can also be made in shapes like rings, or thin cylinders like pencils. These magnets are made from materials called ferrites, which contain iron. Electromagnets are often shaped like thick flat plates, although they can be other shapes.

Horseshoe magnet

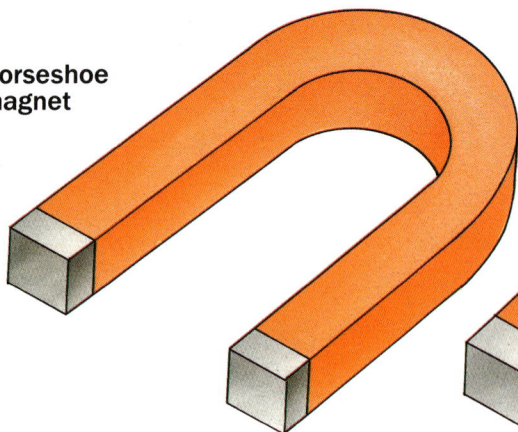

Bar magnet

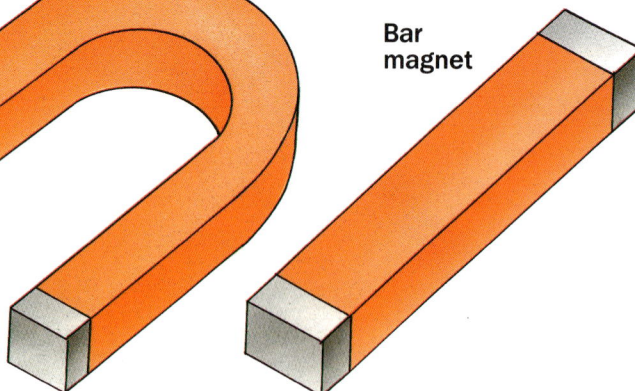

Electro-magnet

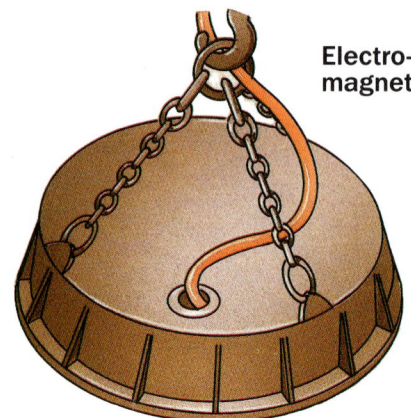

WHAT CAN A MAGNET ATTRACT?

If you play with a magnet, you will notice that not all things are attracted to it. Materials that are attracted to a magnet are called magnetic materials. Other materials are called non-magnetic.

See which of these things are attracted to a magnet: a pin, a paperclip, a plastic knitting needle, a piece of paper, kitchen foil, different kinds of coins, a pencil, and a drinking glass.

You will find that objects made of iron, or containing iron, are attracted to a magnet. Most other metals, such as the aluminium in kitchen foil or the copper in coins, are not attracted.

Glass is not attracted to a magnet

Quiz

Magnets are very useful around the home. They are sometimes used to keep doors closed. When you close a refrigerator door, what makes it close tight? A strip of magnet round the door opening holds the steel door shut. Magnets are also used to keep chess pieces on the board. Do any of the gadgets listed below use magnets? — telephone, cassette recorder, vacuum cleaner, refrigerator, washing machine, radio, television set and home computer. Can you find other magnets in your home?

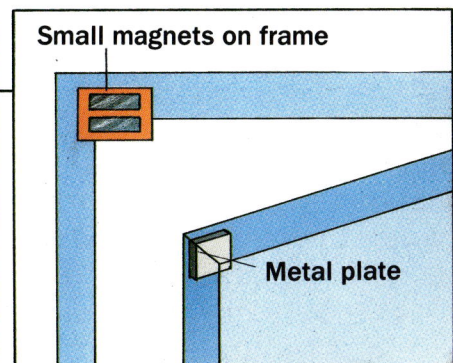

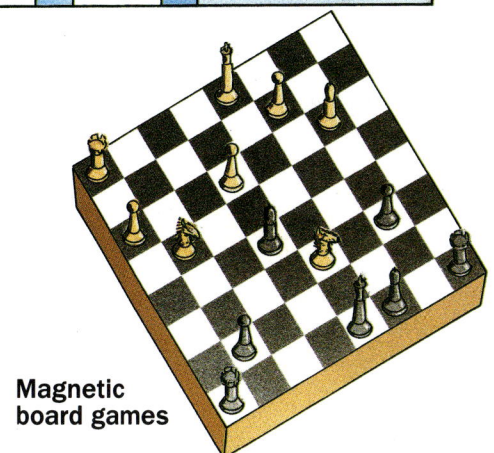

Small magnets on frame

Metal plate

Magnetic door catch

Magnetic board games

Magnets are used in many household gadgets. Electric motors use magnets and motors are used in many appliances, such as vacuum cleaners. A cassette recorder uses tiny magnets on the tape to store sounds. In a television set, magnets are used to move the electron beam which makes the picture.

MEASURING SPEED

A speedometer is driven by a cable that is connected to the wheels of the car or lorry. The cable rotates, or turns round, very rapidly as the vehicle moves along. Inside the speedometer, the cable is attached to a small magnet. The magnet is turned round by the rotating cable. The magnet is inside a flat metal cup which is connected to the pointer on the speedometer dial. As the magnet turns around, it attracts the metal cup, causing the cup to turn. This turns the speedometer pointer, and shows the speed on a dial — the faster the magnet spins, the more the pointer moves.

NO BURGLARS, PLEASE!

A magnet can be used in a burglar alarm, and will sound when a window is opened by an intruder. In many burglar alarms a magnet is fitted onto the window pane. A special switch is then fitted to the frame of the window. When the window is closed, the magnet is near the switch. The magnet attracts a metal bar inside the switch, keeping the bar pressed against an electrical contact, or wire, connected to an electric bell. This stops the bell from ringing. If the window is opened, the magnet moves away from the switch and cannot attract the metal bar. A small spring pulls the bar away from the electrical contact. This breaks the electrical circuit and causes the bell to ring, sounding the alarm.

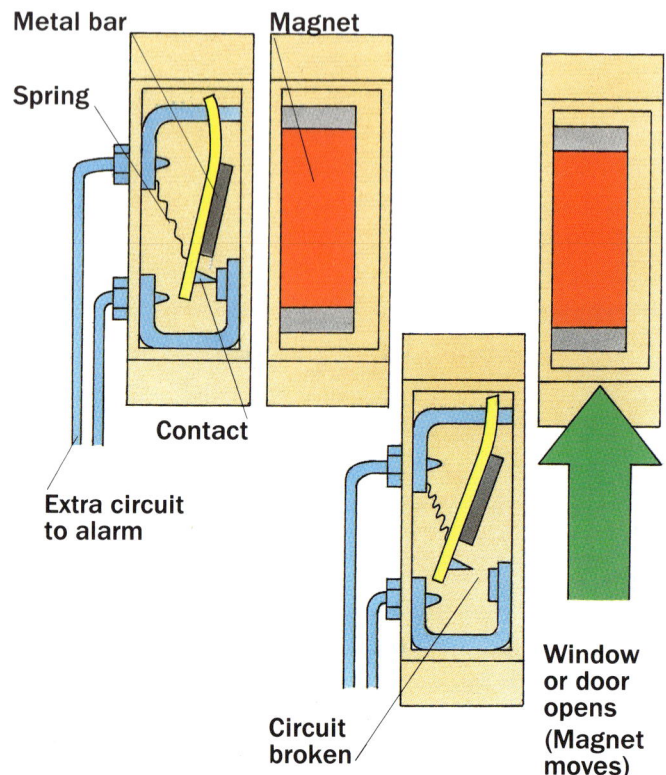

▲ The speedometer is an instrument which shows how fast a car is moving. It works with a magnet that spins around as the car moves.

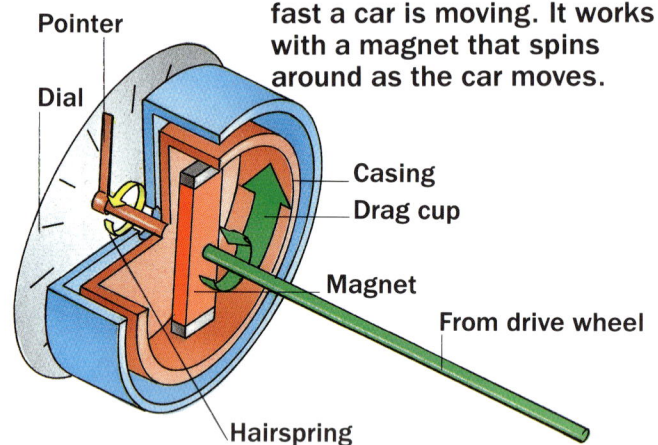

Pointer

Dial

Casing

Drag cup

Magnet

From drive wheel

Hairspring

Metal bar

Magnet

Spring

Contact

Extra circuit to alarm

Circuit broken

Window or door opens (Magnet moves)

COIN TESTER

When a coin is put into a vending machine, an electric current passes through the coin. Only the correct coins conduct the right amount of electricity and are accepted by the machine. Other coins are rejected. The coin then rolls by a magnet which attracts it, slowing it down.

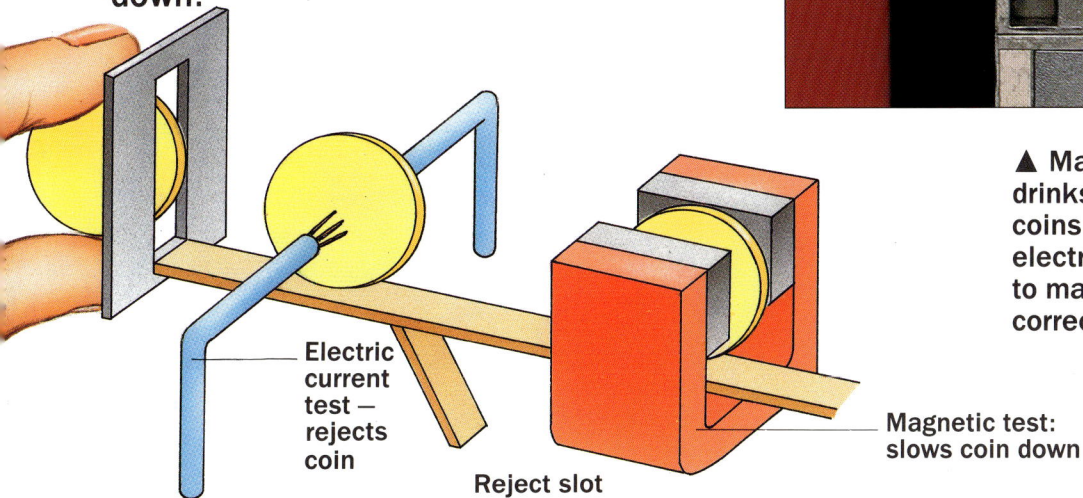

Electric current test — rejects coin

Reject slot

Magnetic test: slows coin down

▲ Machines that sell tickets, drinks or sweets check the coins put in. They use electrical and magnetic tests to make sure the coins are the correct ones.

MAKE A BURGLAR ALARM

You can make a model burglar alarm using simple equipment. You will need a strong magnet, a small electric torch bulb in a holder, a torch battery, drawing pins, thick cardboard, wire and string, all connected together as shown in the diagram. You can use sticky tape to make the connections but metal must touch metal. The magnet is tied to the door, so that it is pulled away when the door is opened. The bent cardboard strip will topple over, completing the electrical circuit. The bulb will light up.

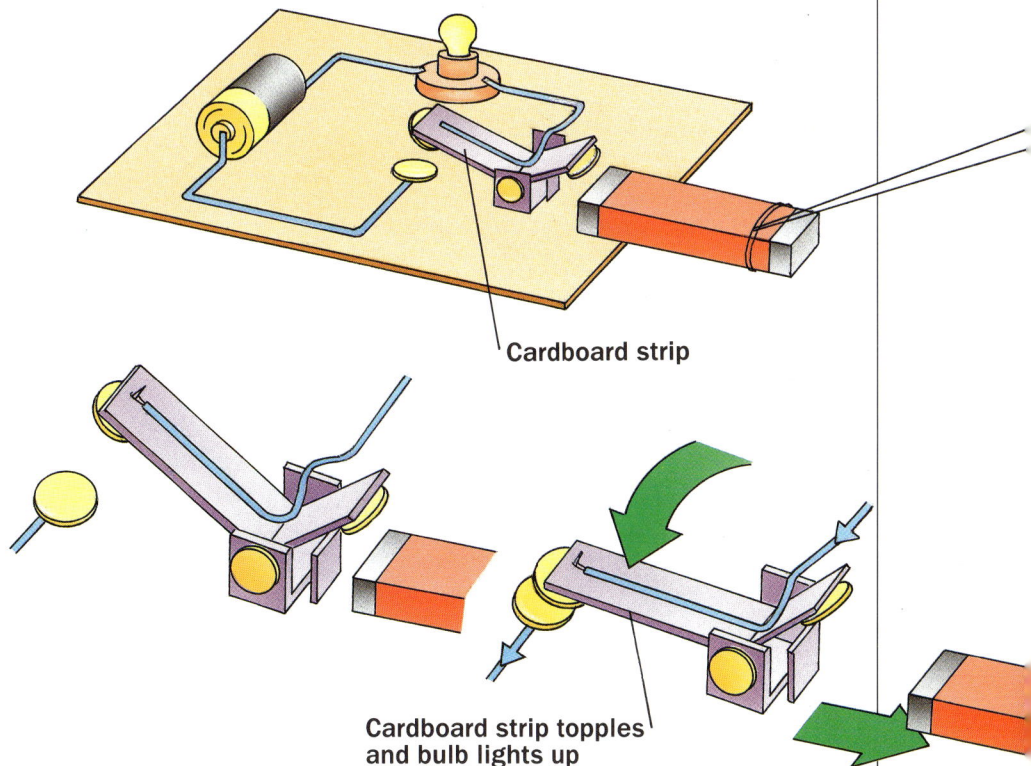

Cardboard strip

Cardboard strip topples and bulb lights up

Not all magnets are the same strength. You can see this if you experiment with different magnets. One magnet might be able to pick up many paperclips or pins. Another might be able to pick up only a few. The magnets used in industry, or by scientists in their experiments, often need to be very strong.

LOCKING MAGNETS

Magnets need to be treated carefully or they will lose their magnetic power. When you finish experimenting with a magnet, place a small piece of metal over the ends. The metal piece is called a keeper. If you have two magnets, place them side by side, and then put the keeper over the ends. Using keepers like this is called "locking" the magnets. Locking a magnet prevents it from losing its magnetism.

▲ Magnets should be joined with keepers when not being used. This helps to conserve their strength.

Unlocked magnets

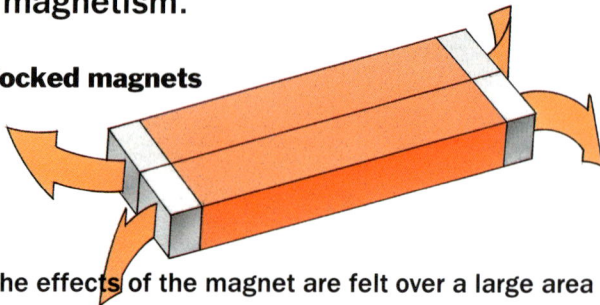

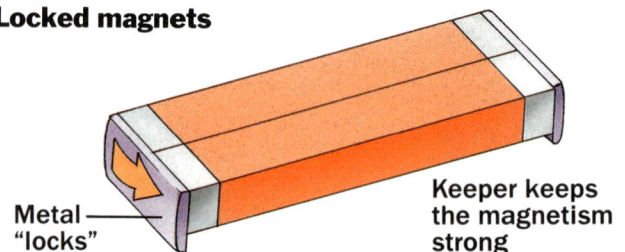

The effects of the magnet are felt over a large area

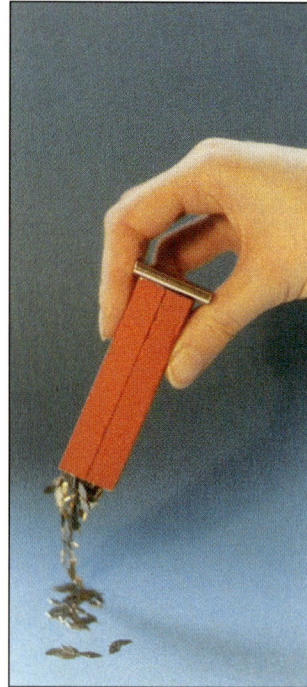

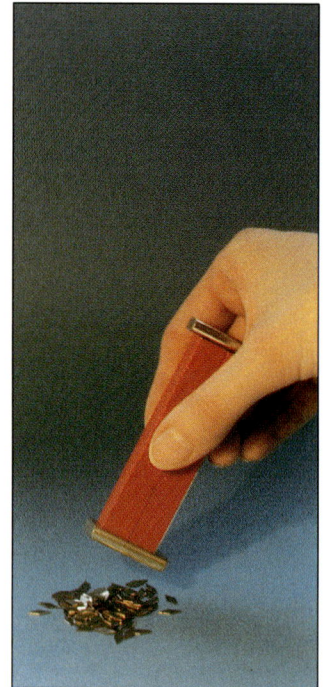

Locked magnets

Metal "locks"

Keeper keeps the magnetism strong

INDUSTRIAL MAGNETS

The magnets used in industry need to stay very strong. Most permanent magnets are made from steel or mixtures of iron with other metals. One common alloy, or mixture of metals, is called alnico. This name shows that the alloy is made from aluminium, nickel and cobalt, as well as iron and sometimes copper and titanium. Alnico alloys can be made into very strong magnets — 30 times stronger than permanent magnets made from other materials. These magnets are used in electrical instruments and appliances. Samarium-cobalt magnets have become important in small, powerful motors.

▲ The photograph shows the use of industrial magnets to separate different types of metal.

INDUCED MAGNETISM

When a paperclip, or any small piece of iron or steel, is attracted to a magnet, the clip itself becomes a magnet. You can see this by arranging paperclips on a magnet. Each paperclip becomes a magnet and attracts other clips. This type of magnetism is called "induced" magnetism.

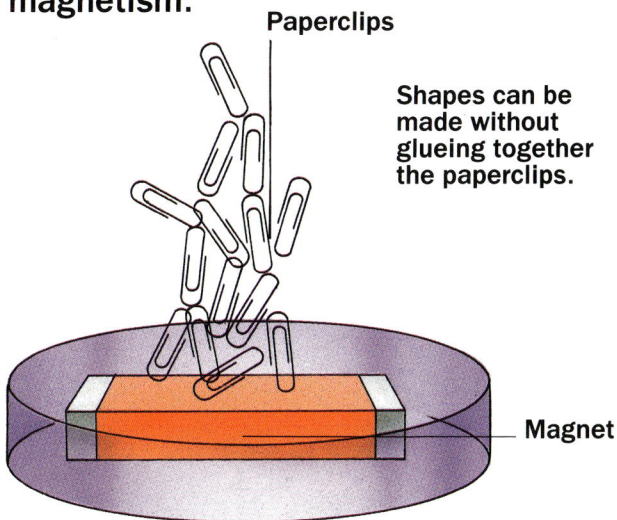

▼ This toy is made from a magnet and metal pieces which become induced magnets and cling to each other.

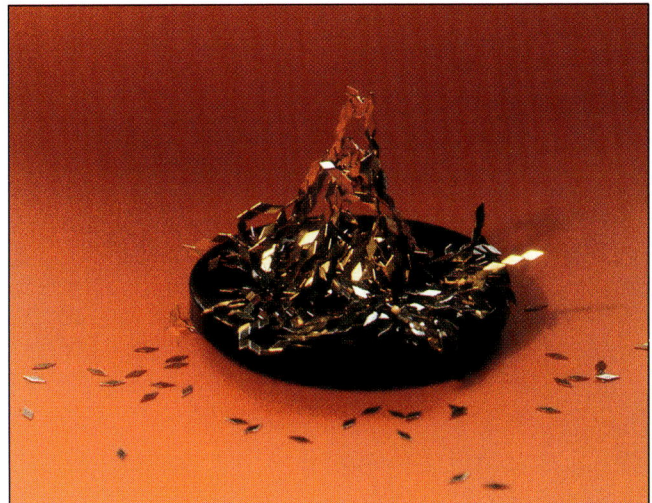

Paperclips

Shapes can be made without glueing together the paperclips.

Magnet

CAN YOU BLOCK A MAGNET'S POWER ?

Can a magnet attract a drawing pin through water? You can find out with a magnet, a glass bowl of water and a drawing pin.

Place a nail on one side of a sheet of paper and move a magnet on the other side. Does the nail move or is the magnet blocked?

Repeat the experiment with a wooden, glass and plastic sheet. You could also try it with a magnetic metal sheet.

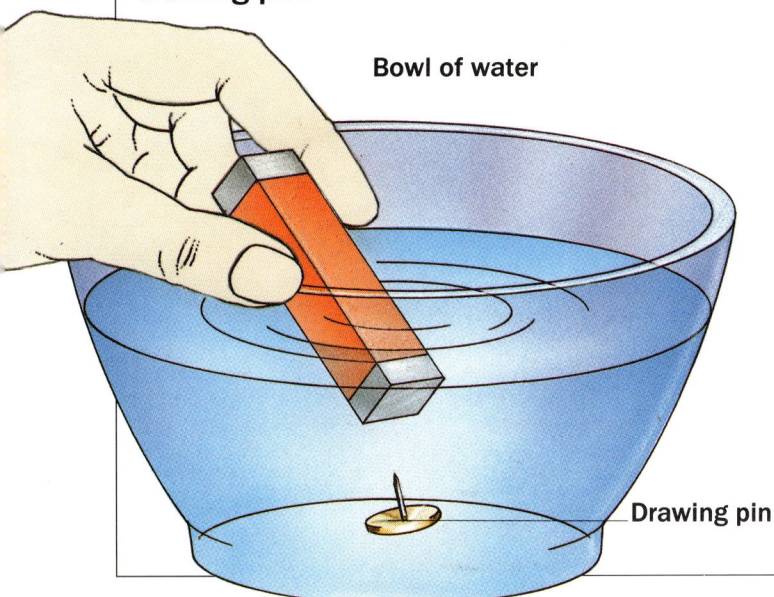

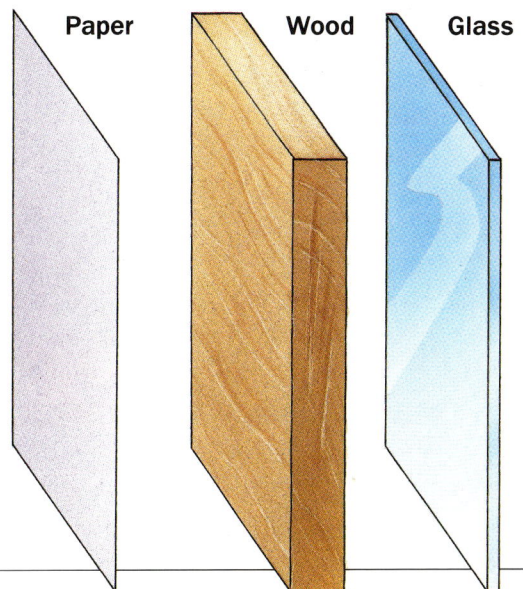

Bowl of water

Drawing pin

Paper

Wood

Glass

The power of a magnet is strongest at two points, called the poles. The poles are usually near the ends of the magnet. They are called the north pole and the south pole. If a magnet is hung on a thread so that it can swing freely, the north pole points to the north. The south pole points south.

ATTRACTION AND REPULSION

If you have two magnets, you will notice that they do not always attract each other. Magnets only attract each other if a north pole is near a south pole. If two of the same poles are placed close together, the magnets push apart, or repel each other. Scientists have made up a rule to describe this. They say: Like poles repel, unlike poles attract. If the magnets are very powerful, it may be impossible to make like poles touch. This principle of attraction and repulsion is used in many machines.

THE MAGLEV TRAIN

The word "maglev" stands for "magnetic levitation", or floating in the air using magnets. The maglev train is a train without wheels. It floats above the track using magnets. Maglev trains are fast, quiet and cause no pollution as they run. But they do need special track which is costly to build. The train shown here has electromagnets underneath. When the magnets are turned on, they are attracted to the iron or steel suspension rail. This lifts the train off the track. In some systems, the suspension rail is made up of permanent magnets that attract the electromagnets. The train is driven along the track by a linear motor. This type of motor has an electromagnet as poles that move along the train. As the poles move, they are attracted to the iron or steel reaction rail and the train is dragged along.

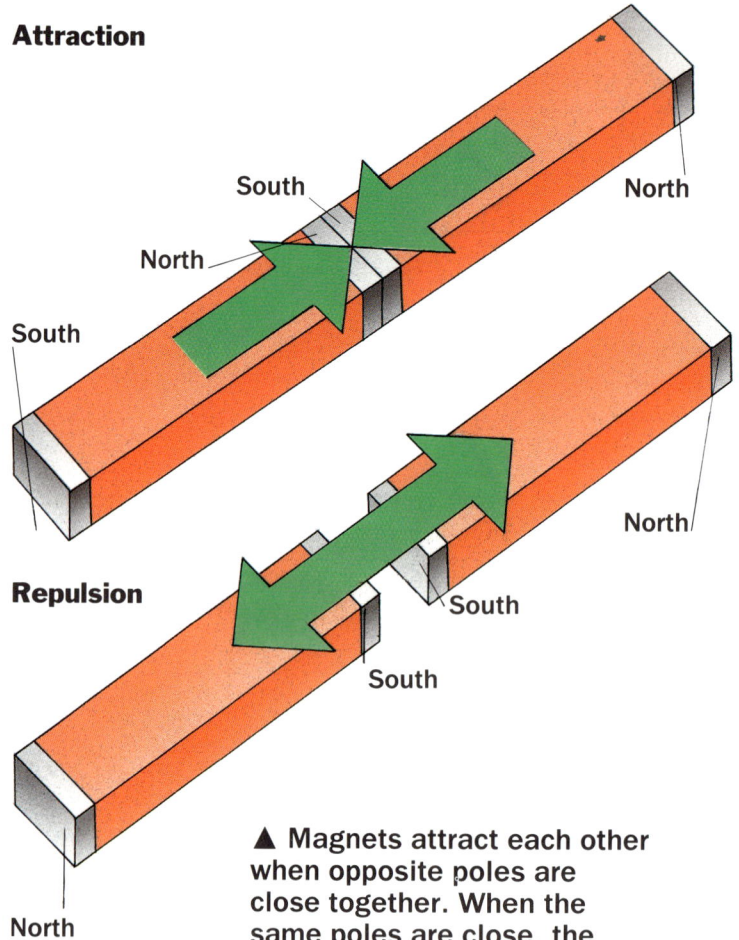

Attraction

South
North
North
South
North

Repulsion

North
South
South

▲ Magnets attract each other when opposite poles are close together. When the same poles are close, the magnets repel.

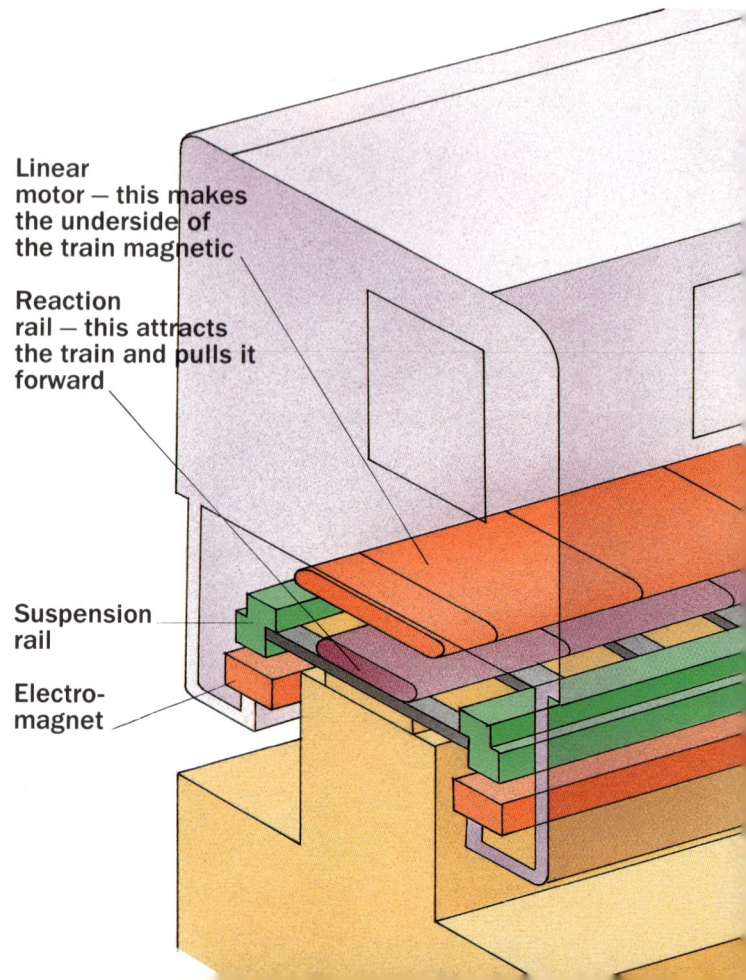

Linear motor — this makes the underside of the train magnetic

Reaction rail — this attracts the train and pulls it forward

Suspension rail

Electro-magnet

DO-IT-YOURSELF MAGLEV

If you have two strong magnets, you can show your friends how maglev works. Place one magnet on top of the other, with the two north poles together. Put a pencil between the magnets. Now tape the sides of the magnets together with flexible sticky tape. Remove the pencil, leaving a space between the magnets. Place the magnets on a table so that one magnet floats above the other. Press down on the top magnet, to feel the "spring" of the magnetic force of the magnets.

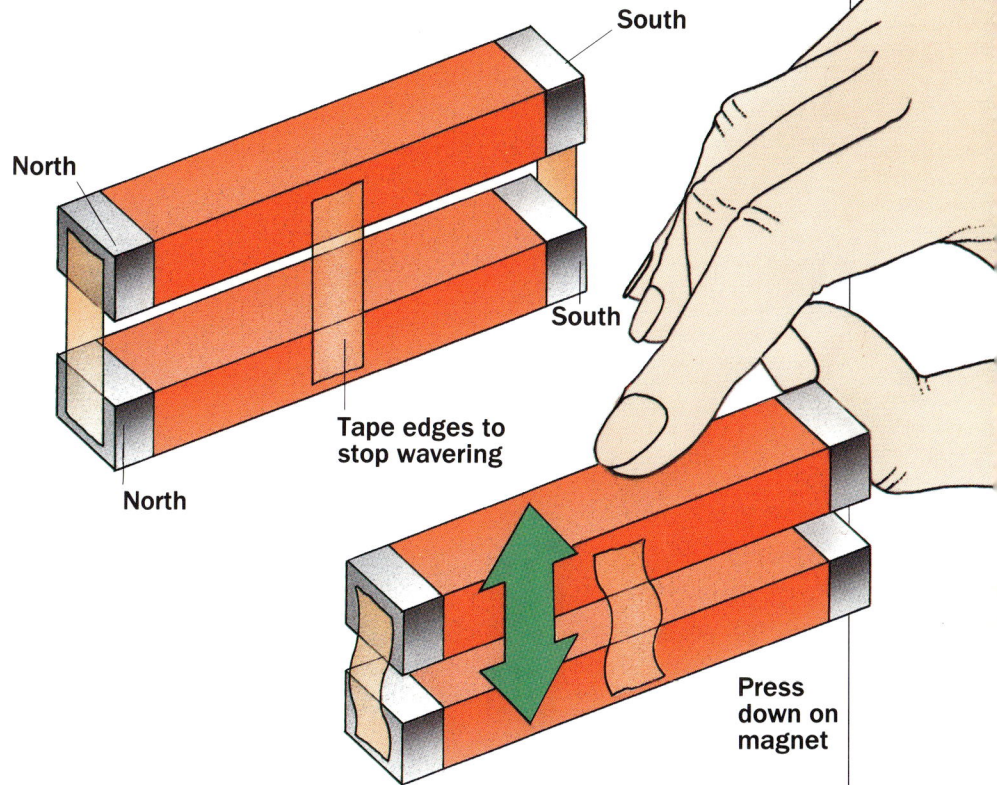

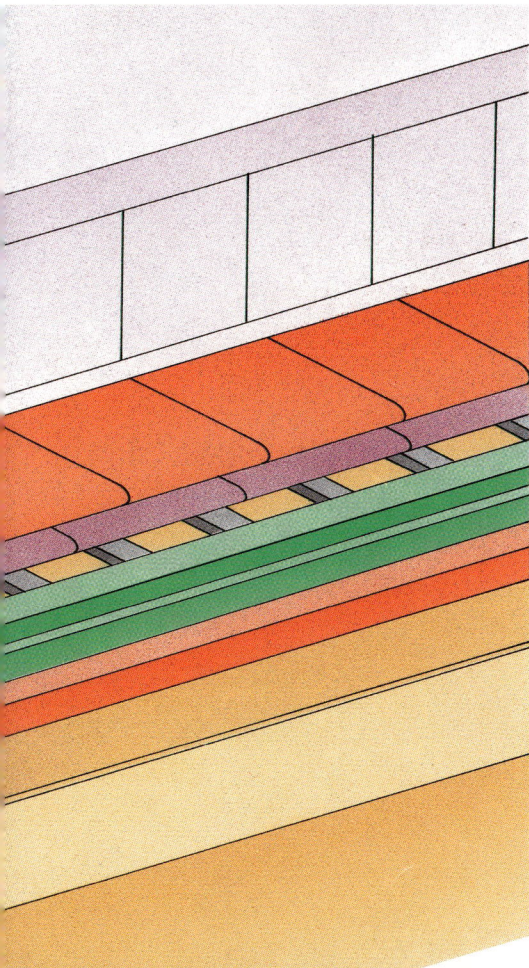

South

North

South

Tape edges to stop wavering

North

Press down on magnet

▲ Maglev trains are fast and the track is expensive to build. They are used only for short journeys in Japan.

If you hold a pin near a magnet, you can feel the magnet attracting the pin. Scientists describe this by saying there is a magnetic field around the magnet. A magnetic field is the space around a magnet where you can feel the force of the magnet on the pin. The magnetic field is strongest close to the magnet.

LINES OF FORCE

A pattern of imaginary lines can be used to describe a magnetic field. These lines are called lines of force. They provide a kind of picture of the magnetic field around a magnet. Lines of force show the direction of the magnetic force near a magnet. They are drawn so that they always run from the north pole of a magnet to the south pole. They are closest together near the poles where the magnetic force is strong. Away from the poles, where the magnetic force is weaker, the lines are further apart so as to show this.

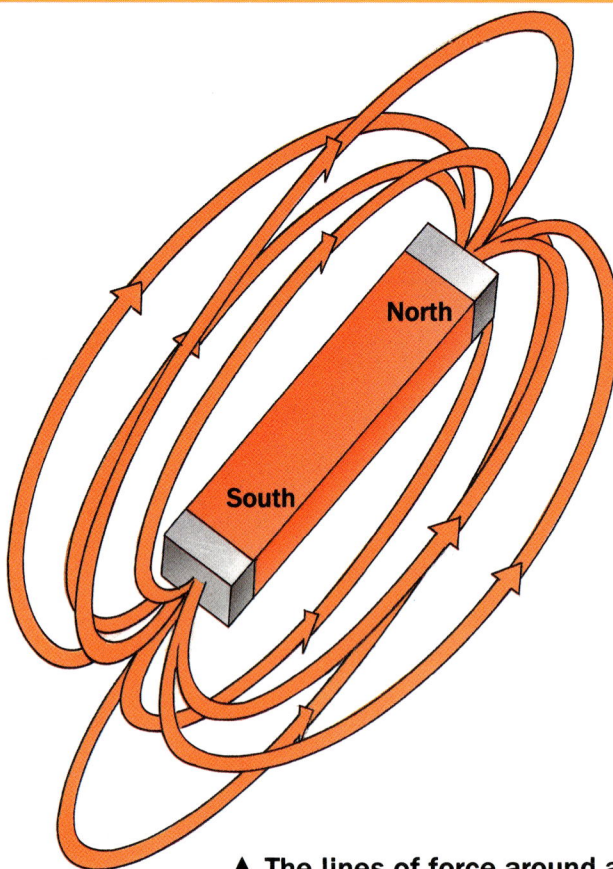

▲ The lines of force around a magnet show where the magnetic force is strongest. They also show the direction of the magnetic force.

SEE LINES OF FORCE FOR YOURSELF

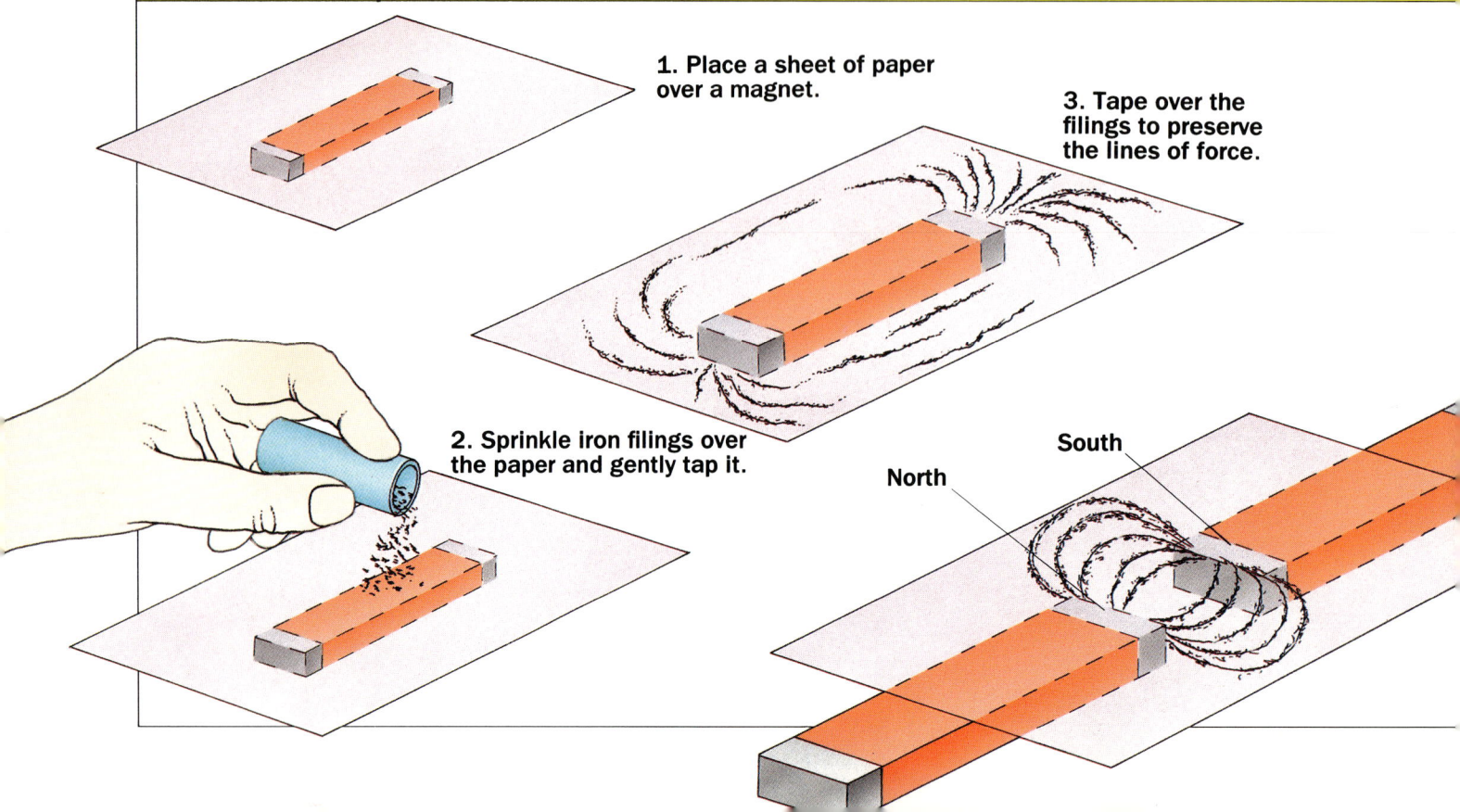

1. Place a sheet of paper over a magnet.

2. Sprinkle iron filings over the paper and gently tap it.

3. Tape over the filings to preserve the lines of force.

North

South

MAGNETIC ANIMALS

Some animals have a built-in magnet that acts like a "compass" and helps them to find their way. Birds use the Earth's magnetic field to navigate when they migrate. If a magnet is fixed to a pigeon's back, the bird becomes confused and cannot find its way on cloudy days. Many whales, dolphins and porpoises follow the Earth's magnetic field when they migrate across the oceans. Some snails have magnets on their tongues which they use to find their way home. These snails always point north when they are resting. Compass termites from Australia always build their nests pointing to the north. Perhaps they use the Earth's magnetism to line up their mounds. Even humans have a built-in compass. There is magnetic material just behind your nose! Scientists know this because blindfolded people taken many kilometres from home can find their way back more accurately than people without a blindfold.

▲ Migrating birds have built-in compasses that they use for navigation. Changes in the magnetic field of the Sun can make them lose their sense of direction.

You can reveal the positions of lines of force around a magnet by using iron filings. These are small pieces of iron, about the size of salt grains. Place a sheet of paper over a magnet and sprinkle the filings onto the paper. Tap the paper gently, and the filings will arrange themselves in lines in the magnetic field. Repeat the experiment with two magnets under the paper. Put two north poles close together, and then a north pole near a south pole.

WHAT HAPPENS HERE?

What pattern of filings would you expect to occur around a horseshoe magnet? Remember that the magnetic field is strongest near the poles. Repeat the experiment on the left with iron filings, a sheet of paper and two horseshoe magnets. When the magnets attract each other, you will be able to feel how the magnetic force pulls them together and see the pattern of filings. When the magnets repel each other, you will be able to see how the pattern of filings changes and feel how the magnets push each other apart.

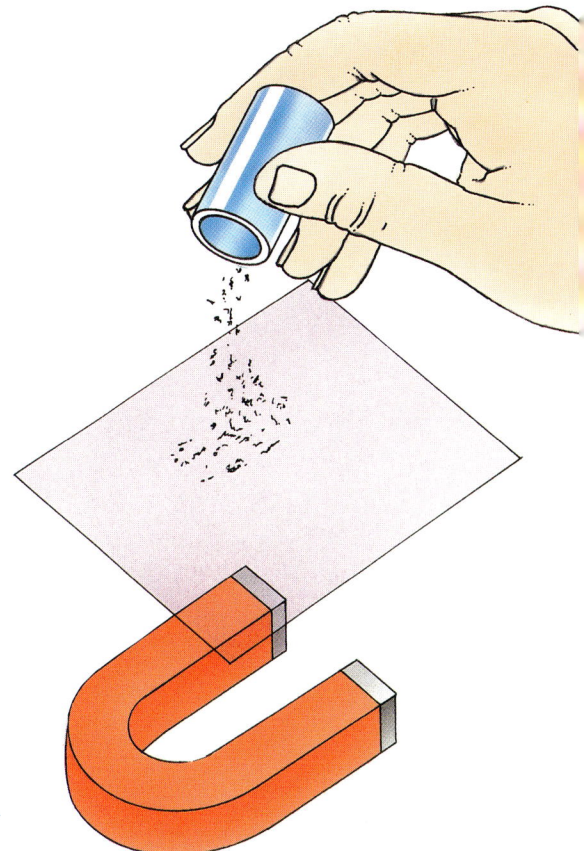

The best-known use of a magnet is to help travellers find their way. The Chinese were using magnets in this way in the 11th century. They used a magnetic needle stuck through a straw floating in a bowl of water. The needle turned to point north and south. Similar compasses were introduced to Europe in around 1200.

ALWAYS NORTH

The Earth behaves like a giant magnet with a magnetic field surrounding it. The magnetic field of the Earth is produced by the molten metal which is found deep below the Earth's surface, at the core or centre of the Earth. As the Earth spins, electric currents are created in the molten metal. These currents produce the Earth's magnetic field. The field produced is like the field of a bar magnet with one pole in northern Canada. This is called the north magnetic pole. The south magnetic pole is in the Antarctic. A compass needle points to the north and south magnetic poles.

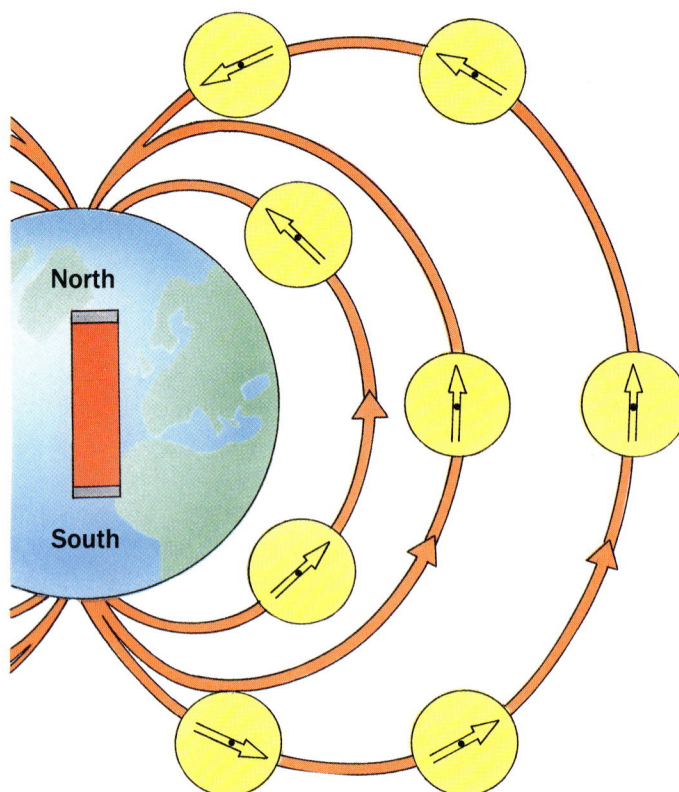

▲ Compasses point in the direction of the magnetic field surrounding the Earth, towards the magnetic poles.

REAL NORTH?

The Earth's true, or geographic, poles lie at the ends of the axis on which it rotates once a day. The north magnetic pole is about 1,600 kilometres away from the true North Pole. The south magnetic pole is about 2,400 kilometres from the true South Pole. It is as if the imaginary bar magnet inside the Earth is slightly tilted to one side. The angle between the direction a compass points and true north is called the magnetic declination or variation. Navigators using compasses have to remember this when they work out the direction of true north. Scientists studying old rocks have found that the Earth's magnetic poles — move a few centimetres each year. They have also found that the strength of the Earth's magnetism changes slowly.

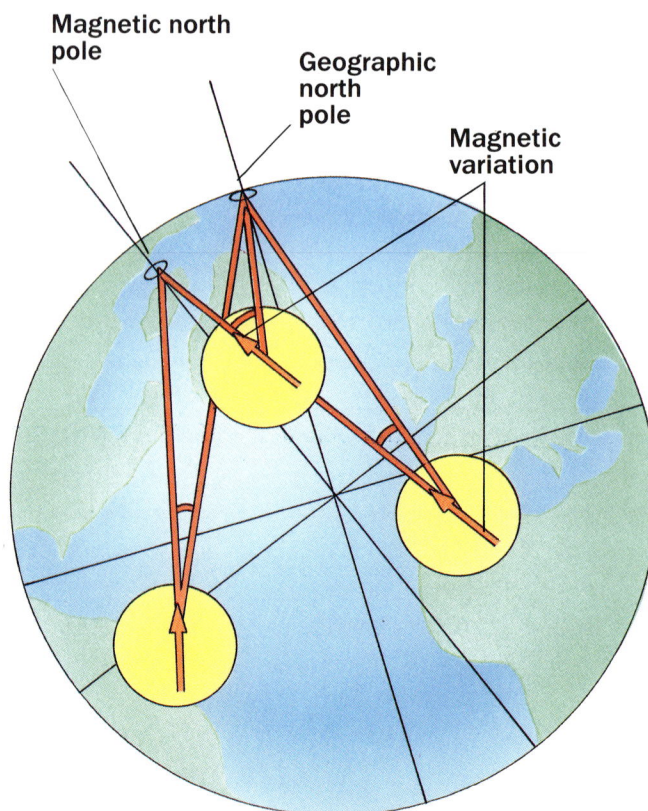

Magnetic north pole

Geographic north pole

Magnetic variation

THE MODERN COMPASS

A modern compass, such as those used by hikers, has a thin needle balanced on a fine point so that it can turn easily. Below the needle is a card marked with the points of the compass, north, east, south and west. A ship's compass has a card, marked with points of the compass, instead of a needle. On the underside of the card are strips of magnetised metal. The card floats in a bowl of liquid. The bowl is mounted so that it remains steady in rough weather. This means that the compass gives accurate readings in stormy seas.

Small magnetised needle

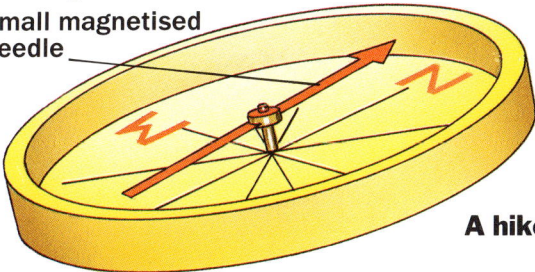

A hiker's compass

▲ In the sport of orienteering, runners must find their way in rough country using a compass.

MAKE YOUR OWN COMPASS

Make a compass from a bar magnet and some thread. Tie one end of the thread around the magnet. Make sure the magnet is balanced when it is hung from the thread. If you have a thin magnetised needle, you can make a water compass. Cut about 3 centimetres from a drinking straw. Push the needle through the centre of the straw, at right-angles to it. Plug the ends of the straw with play dough. Put the straw and needle in a bowl of water. The magnet will turn to point north-south.

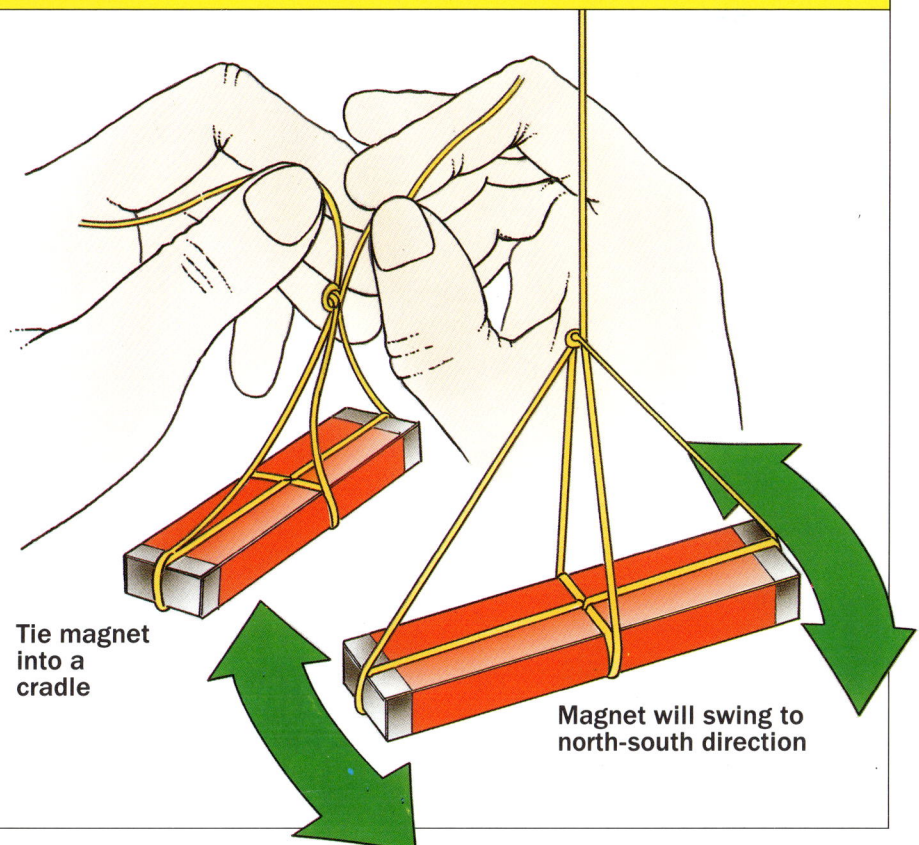

Tie magnet into a cradle

Magnet will swing to north-south direction

There are a number of simple ways of making a magnet. The best-known way is by stroking an iron or steel bar with a lodestone, or magnet. Another, more complicated, way of making a magnet is to heat an iron bar, then point the bar to the north and hit it with a hammer. These magnets are permanent magnets.

ALL IN LINE

To understand why hitting an iron bar creates a magnet you have to remember that an iron or steel bar, is made up of tiny particles called atoms. In a magnetic material like iron or steel, the atoms are magnetic. Groups of atoms, called domains, combine and act like miniature magnets. When the needle is unmagnetised, the domains are pointing in different directions, cancelling each other out. However, when an iron bar is stroked with a magnet, the domains are attracted by the magnet. They become lined up so that they all point in the same direction. Their magnetism then combines to turn the bar into a magnet.

Non-magnet

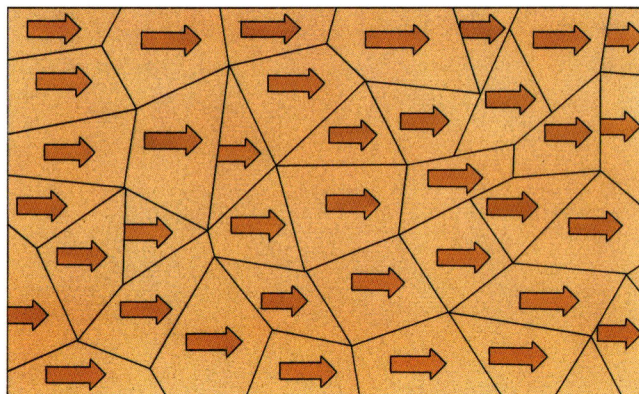

Magnet

▲ In an unmagnetised iron or steel bar, the domains point in all directions and cancel out. In a magnetised bar, all the domains line up.

MAKING MAGNETS

In industry, permanent magnets are made by electrically magnetising metal rods. The rods are made of special alloys, such as alnico or samarium-cobalt. They are placed in a coil of wire carrying an electric current. The magnetic field of the coil affects the rods and makes the magnetic domains in the rods line up — all pointing in the same direction. Magnets with complicated shapes are made by mixing powdered iron with glue. The mixture is placed in a mould, to form the shape, and allowed to dry. Some magnets made in this way are then baked in a hot oven until they become hard. Materials made by baking in an oven are called ferrites. They are used in radios and television sets.

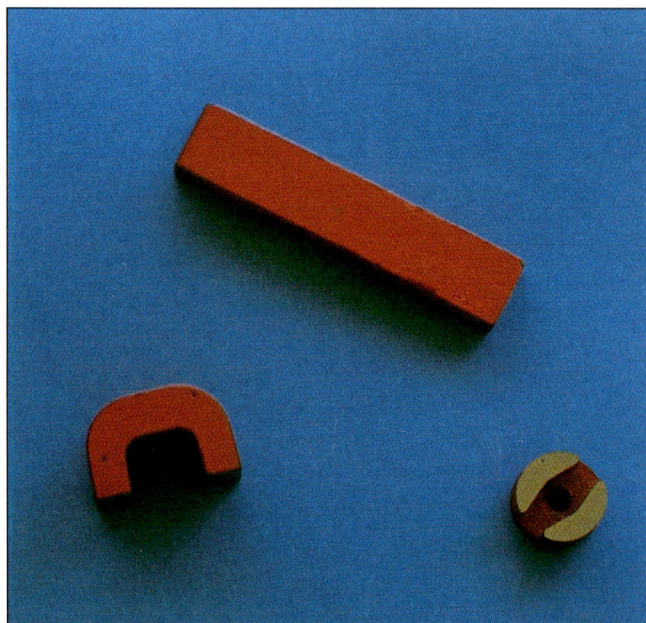

▲ Magnets of different shapes can be made by using a variety of moulds.

BREAKING A MAGNET

Vibration

Always treat a magnet with care. Never let it get too hot. If a magnet is heated, it will lose its magnetism. The heat makes the domains of atoms move about. This means that they no longer line up and eventually they point in all directions and cancel each other out. So the magnet loses its magnetism. A magnet also loses its power if it is hammered, or dropped onto the floor. Hammering or the dropping again disarranges the domains and the magnetism is destroyed. The opposite happens when an unmagnetised iron bar is hammered while pointing north. The Earth's magnetic field pulls the jostled domains into line, and the bar becomes magnetised. However only a weak magnet can be made in this way and its magnetism easily destroyed.

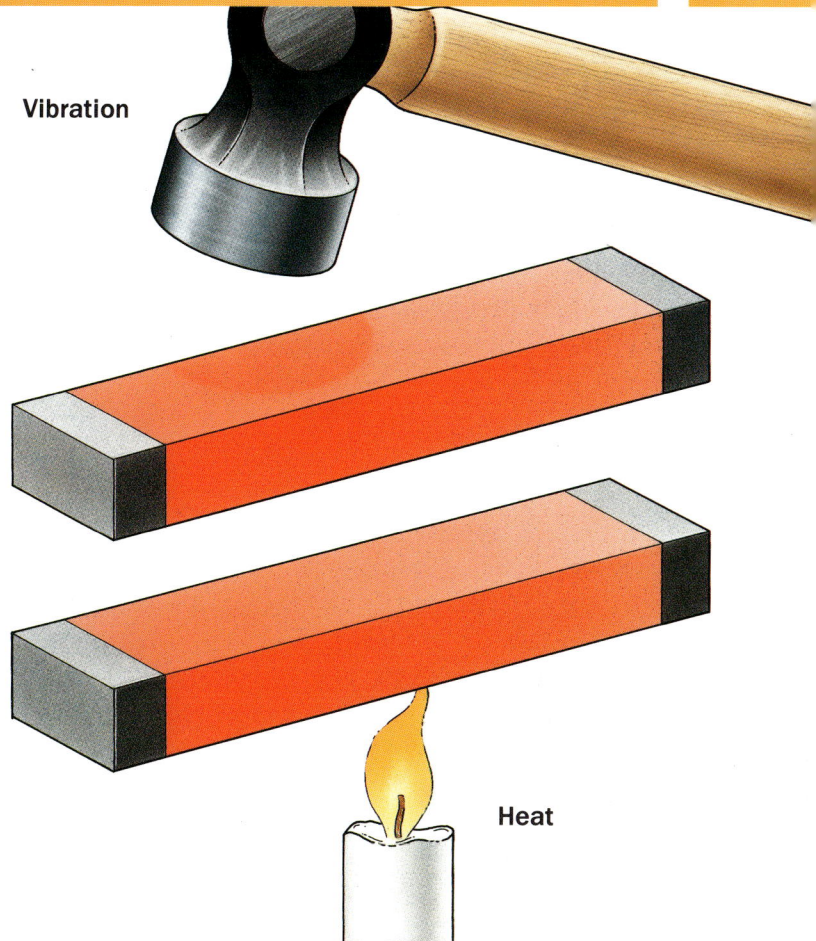

Heat

MAKE YOUR OWN MAGNET

Magnetise a large iron nail by the stroking method. Stroke one pole of a strong magnet along the nail. Lift the magnet away from the nail as you return to the start of the stroke.

You will need to stroke the nail about 50 times. Remember to start at the same pole of the magnet each stroke, and always stroke the same way along the nail.

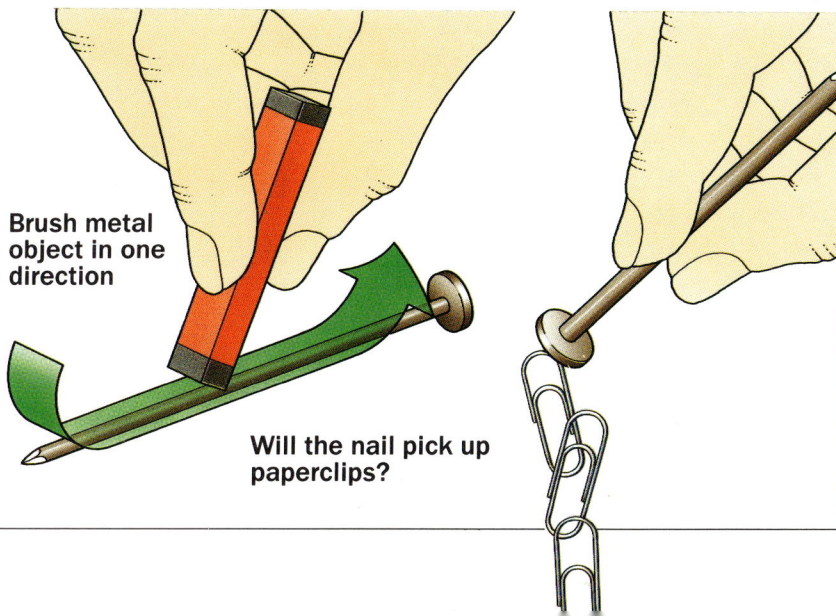

Brush metal object in one direction

Will the nail pick up paperclips?

WHAT HAPPENS?

What happens if a magnet is cut in half? Will each half be a magnet? How many poles will the halves have? The answer is that each half will be a magnet with two poles. This is because, when the magnet is cut, the domains are still lined up in each half.

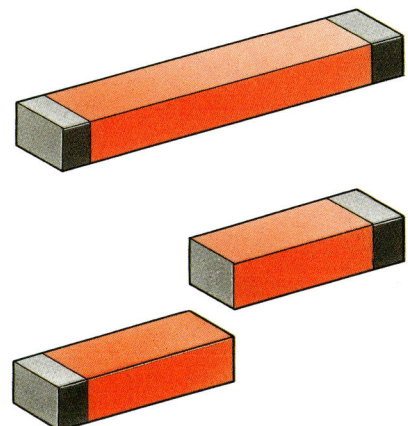

There is a close connection between electric currents and magnetism. Electric currents produce magnetic effects. Magnetism produced in this way is called electromagnetism. Many electrical machines and household appliances such as electric bells and loudspeakers work because of electromagnetism.

CURRENT AND FIELD

You can easily see the effects of the magnetism produced by an electric current. Connect a wire across the terminals of a torch battery. Bring the wire near a small compass needle. The needle will swing to point at right angles to the wire. The current in the wire is producing a magnetic field that is affecting the compass needle. The lines of force drawn around the wire are circular. They form rings around the wire. The magnetic field can be detected if a wire is passed through a card and iron filings scattered on the card. When a strong current flows through the wire, the filings form rings around the wire.

THE MAGNETIC COIL

If the wire carrying an electric current is wound into a coil, the magnetic effect is greater. This can be done by winding a wire around a pencil, and then removing the pencil. A coil of wire made like this is called a solenoid. When an electric current flows through a solenoid, the magnetic field of a solenoid is just like the field of a bar magnet. The lines of force run from one end of the coil and travel to the other end of the coil. The more turns of wire in the coil, the stronger the magnetism produced. Also, the greater the electric current flowing, the greater the magnetic effect. So powerful batteries produce the best effects. When the battery is disconnected from the coil, the magnetism stops.

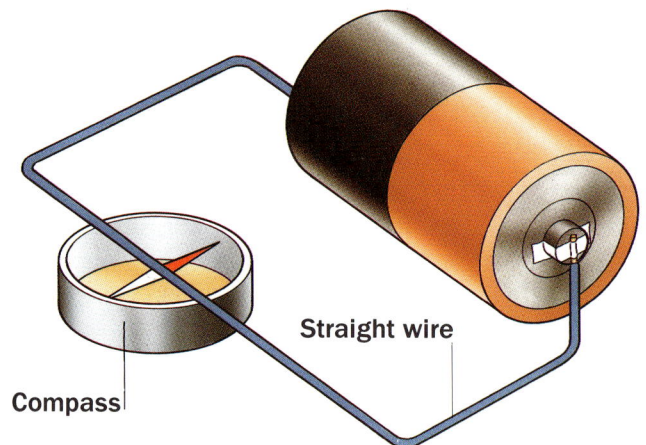

Compass

Straight wire

▲ A compass needle swings to point away from the wire when an electric current flows through the wire.

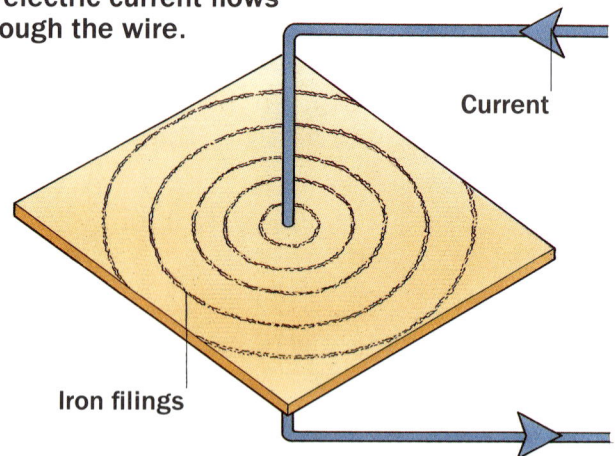

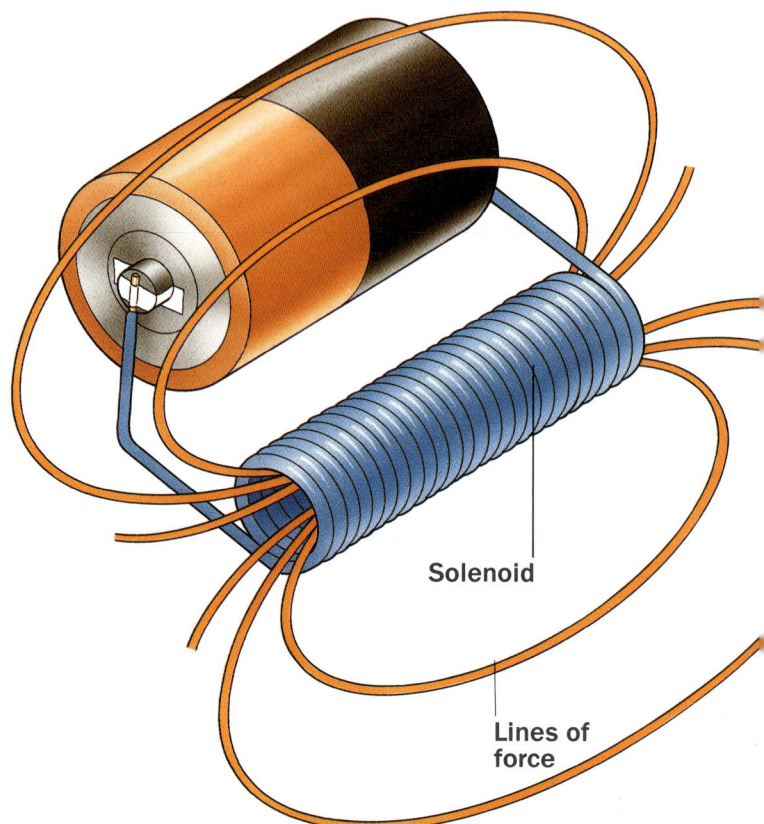

Current

Iron filings

Solenoid

Lines of force

THE POLES OF A COIL

Connect a coil to a battery, and place a compass needle near each end of the coil. You will see that one end of the coil attracts the north pole of the nearby compass needle. At the other end of the coil, the south pole will be attracted. This is because the coil is acting like a bar magnet, with a south pole at one end and a north pole at the other. What will happen if you reverse the connections to the battery? Are the poles reversed?

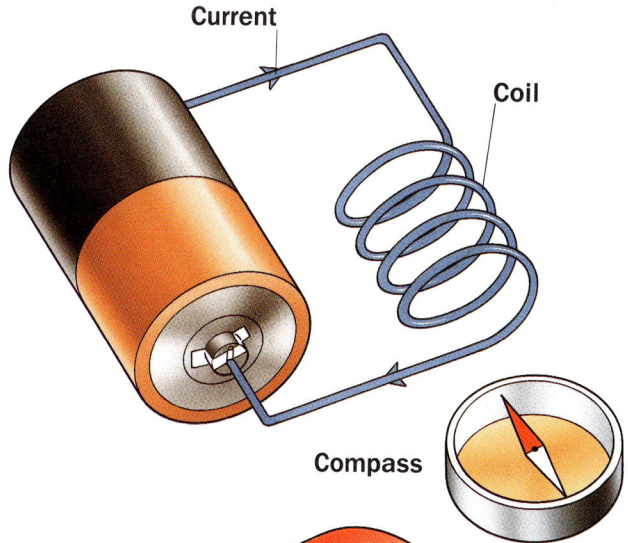

Current

Coil

Compass

MEASURING CURRENT

The size of an electric current is measured with an instrument called a galvanometer. This consists of a small coil of wire between the poles of a permanent magnet. The coil is wrapped around an iron core which can rotate, or turn. When an electric current flows through the coil, the coil becomes magnetic. This causes the coil to turn between the poles of the magnet.

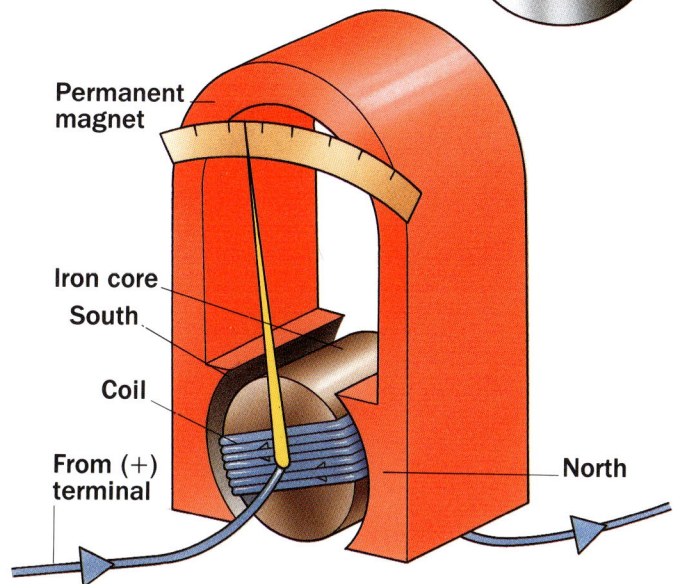

Permanent magnet

Iron core

South

Coil

From (+) terminal

North

MAKE YOUR OWN CURRENT INDICATOR

A simple current indicator can be made with a compass and a coil of wire, as shown in the diagram. Turn the coil and compass until the compass needle lies parallel to the coil. When the ends of the coil are connected to a torch battery, the needle will swing towards the coil. What would happen if you used a larger battery? Would it make the needle swing futher than a small battery?

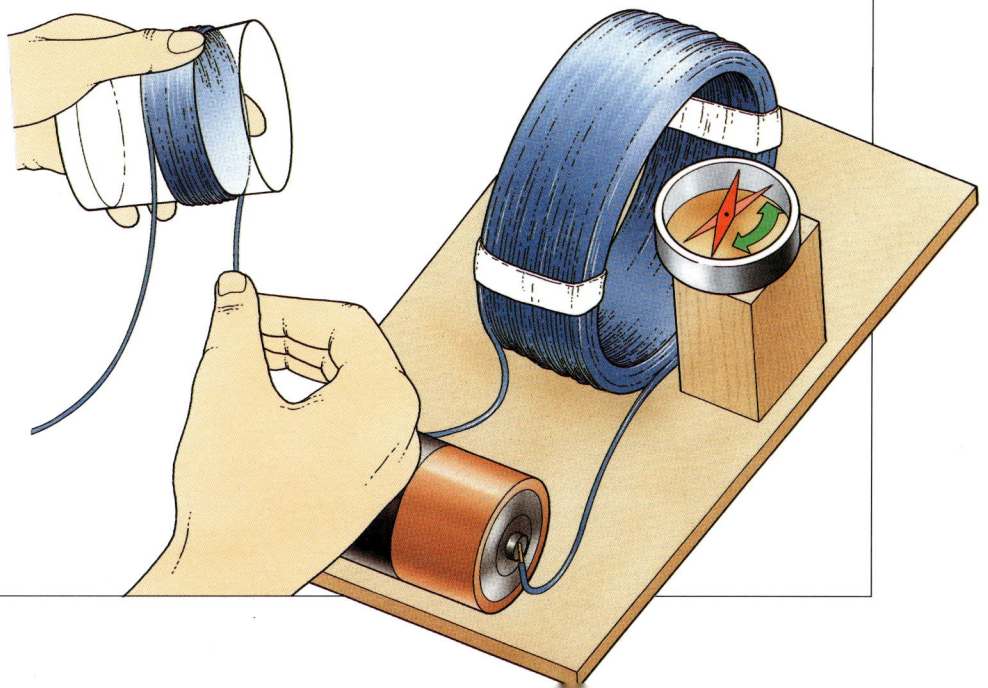

When an iron bar is placed inside a solenoid, the magnetic effect of the coil increases. The lines of force produced by the current-carrying coil flow through the iron, making it into a strong magnet. A magnet made in this way is called an electromagnet. They are useful because they can be turned off and on.

MAKE AN ELECTROMAGNET

An electromagnet can be made by wrapping plastic-covered wire around a steel nail. If you connect the ends of the wire to a battery, the nail will become a magnet and will attract pins and paperclips. If you switch off the current, by disconnecting the battery, you will probably find that the nail still acts as a magnet. This is because steel keeps its magnetism. If, instead of steel, you use soft iron, you will find that the magnetism disappears when the current is turned off. Soft iron does not keep its magnetism like steel. So most electromagnets use soft iron. You can make soft iron by heating a nail to red heat and letting it cool slowly. If you increase the number of turns of wire around the nail, you will find the electromagnet becomes stronger. It will pick up more pins or paperclips. Also, if you connect two batteries, so that a greater current flows through the coil, the magnet becomes stronger.

MODEL RAILWAY SIGNALS

A coil of wire carrying an electric current has another surprising property. An iron or steel nail is attracted into the coil. This effect can be used to make a model railway signal.

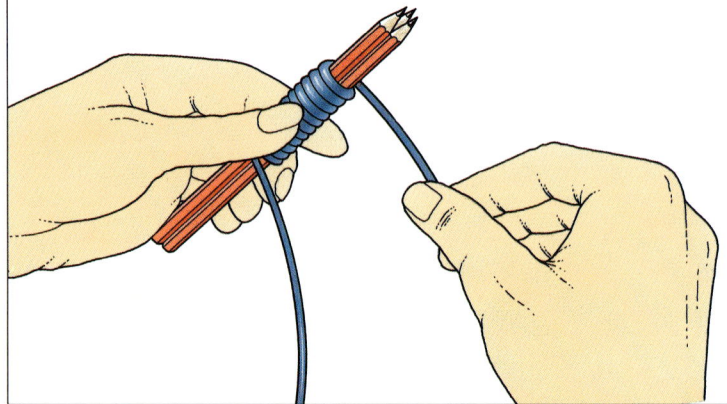

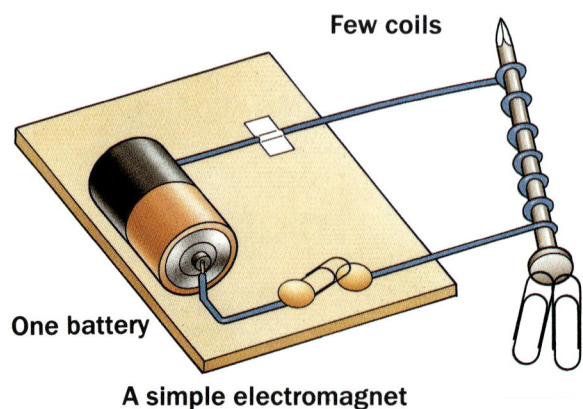

Few coils

One battery

A simple electromagnet

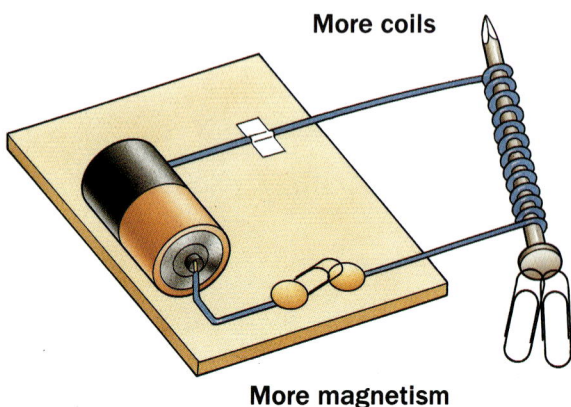

More coils

More magnetism

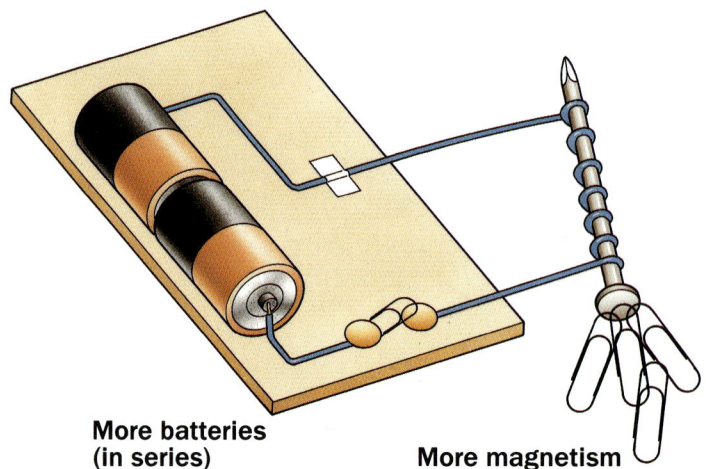

More batteries (in series)

More magnetism

Straw

Bent paperclip

Drawing pins

Coil

Nail

Switch on

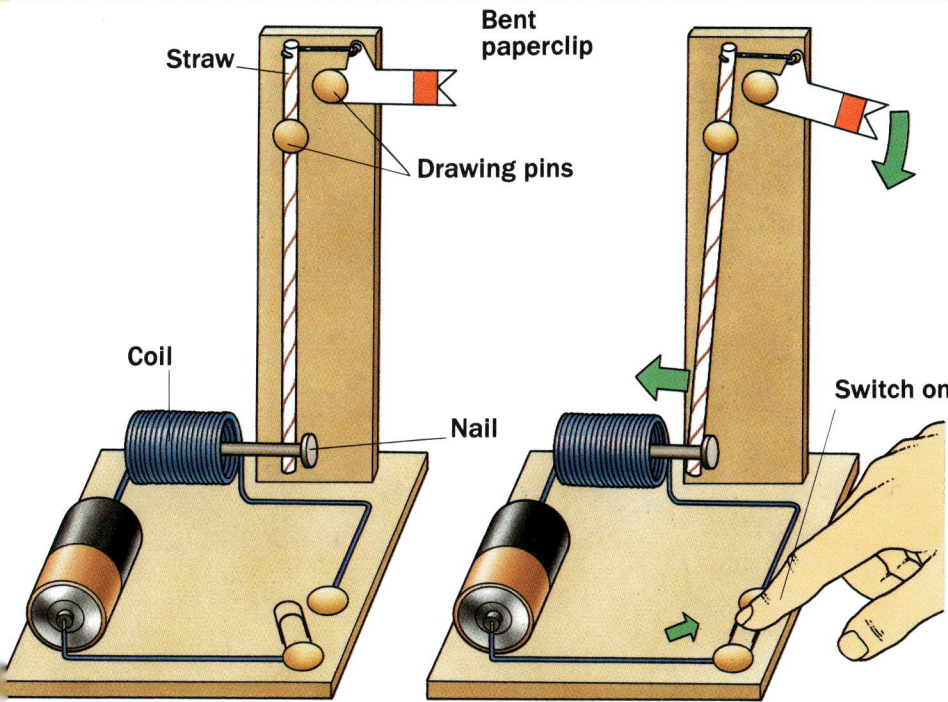

Push a metal nail through one end of a drinking straw. Then glue or nail two pieces of wood together to make an upside down T shape. With pins, attach the straw and nail to the upright piece of wood so that the straw hangs loosely.

Fix a cardboard signal arm to the top of the straw, using cotton and pins as shown. Wind some wire around a pencil to make a coil. Position the coil near the hanging nail, so that the nail is attracted into the coil when the current is turned on. This lifts the signal arm.

DING DONG BELLS

An electric door bell uses an electromagnet. In the type of bell shown, a current flows through the coil when the doorbell button is pressed. This magnetises the soft iron core. The metal chimes are attracted and move towards the core. As each chime hits the core, it produces a musical note. The chimes are different lengths and so produce two different notes, making a "ding dong" sound. The movement of the chimes breaks the electrical circuit and the iron core loses its magnetism. The chimes swing back to their original position. The process repeats as long as the doorbell button is being pressed.

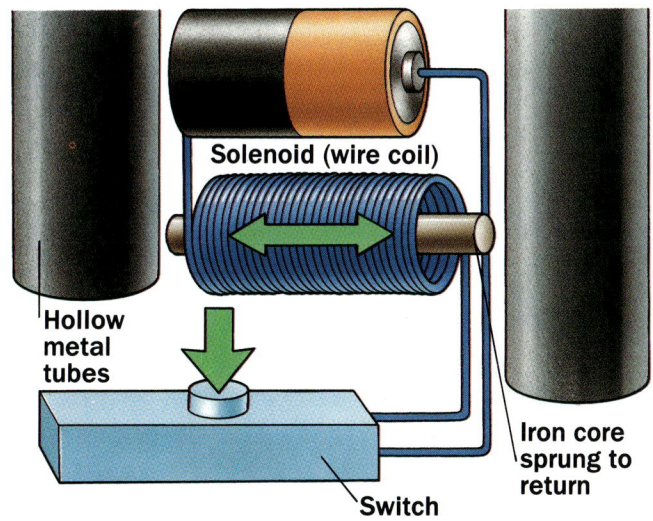

Solenoid (wire coil)

Hollow metal tubes

Iron core sprung to return

Switch

▶ All doorbells use an electromagnet to make a hammer hit against the bell or chime. The movement of the hammer is used to break the electric circuit and keep the bell ringing.

Electromagnets are used in many different ways. They are found in electric motors, video machines, computers, loudspeakers and telephones. In a television set, they are used to control the beams which form the picture. In hospitals, they are used to remove metal splinters from wounds.

THE SCRAPYARD CRANE

An electromagnet's strength and ability to be turned on and off makes it ideal for moving heavy loads of metal in a scrapyard. A powerful electromagnet, hanging from the arm of a crane, is often used. The electromagnet consists of a large coil of wire inside a steel casing. A non-magnetic plate underneath the coil makes sure the magnetic lines of force spread beneath the magnet. The electromagnet is strong enough to lift a scrapped car. When the crane has carried the scrap to the correct spot, the driver turns the electric current in the coil off. The scrap immediately drops to the ground.

THE CAR HORN

A car horn is similar to an electric bell. When the horn button is pressed, an electric current flows through the coil of an electromagnet. The energised electromagnet attracts an iron bar. As the bar moves towards the coil, it pushes the contacts apart. This breaks the electric circuit and the current stops flowing. A spring pulls the bar back to its original position. The contact points close together, and the current starts to flow again. The process repeats. In this way, the bar is made to vibrate rapidly back and forth. The bar is attached to a thin metal sheet, or diaphragm. The diaphragm also vibrates making a loud sound. The sound travels down a horn which concentrates the sound forwards.

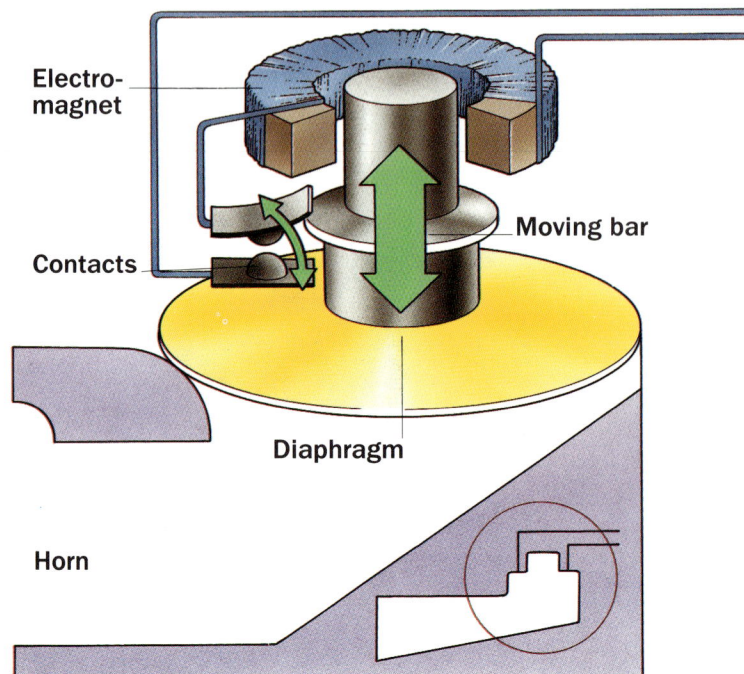

▲ In a scrapyard, electromagnets are used to move metal scrap and also to separate iron and steel from other scrap.

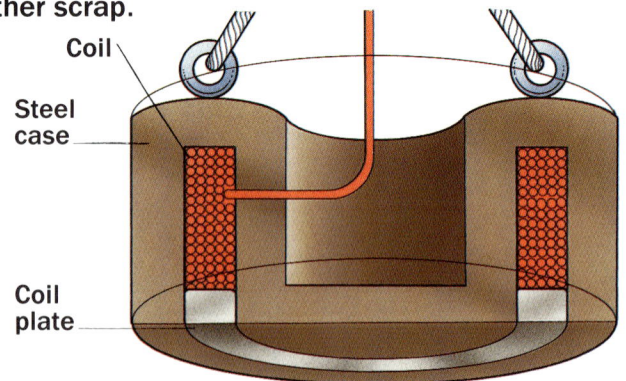

Coil

Steel case

Coil plate

Electro-magnet

Contacts

Moving bar

Diaphragm

Horn

MAKE AN ELECTROMAGNETIC CRANE

You will need: a long steel nail, plastic covered wire, a torch battery, two square cardboard boxes, a cardboard tube, a cotton reel, a pencil, a paperclip, scissors, strong glue, and some thick cardboard to make the crane.

First, cut one of the boxes in half to form the base. Make a hole in the top of the base and insert the cardboard tube. Make a hole in the bottom of the other box. Insert the top of the tube through the hole and glue the tube to the top box as shown.

Cut a piece of thick cardboard to form the arm of the crane. Attach the arm to the cotton reel as shown. Insert the cotton reel inside the top box, with the arm lying in slots cut in the front and the pencil through two holes in the sides.

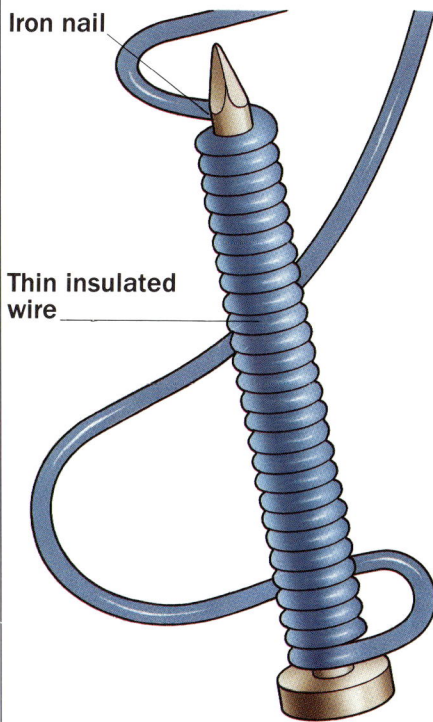

Iron nail

Thin insulated wire

The crane

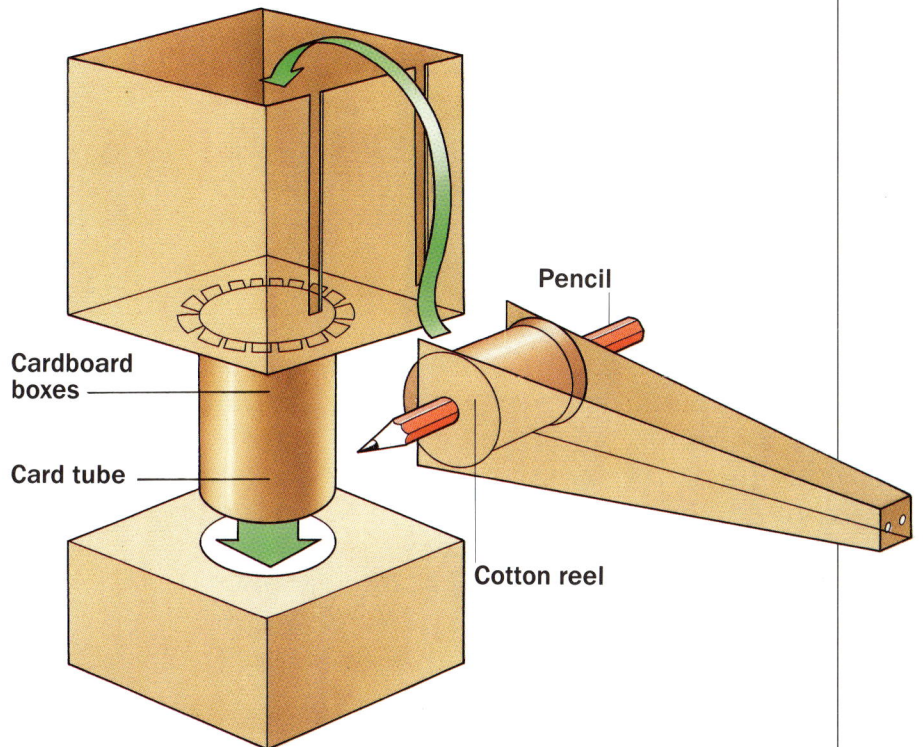

Cardboard boxes

Card tube

Pencil

Cotton reel

OFF

ON

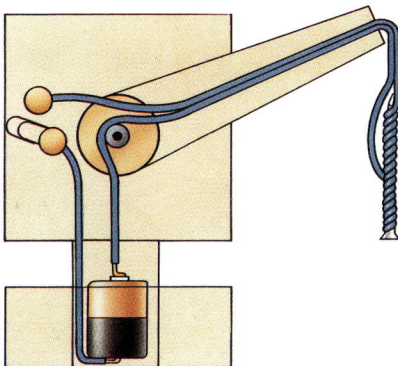

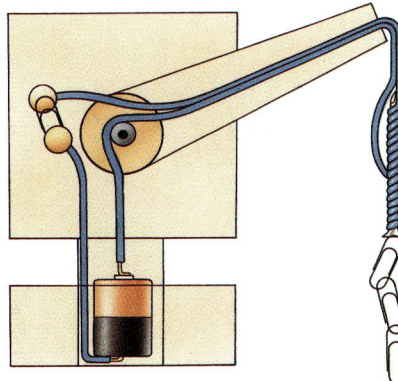

Make a switch on the side of the crane using paper fasteners and a paper clip. Then make an electromagnet by winding about 30 turns of plastic-covered wire around the nail. Connect the battery to the electromagnet and switch as shown.

Tape recorders use magnets to record sounds. A microphone converts the sounds we wish to record into an electrical signal. This signal is stored as a pattern of magnetism on a plastic tape. The tape player reproduces the electrical signal from the pattern. The loudspeaker turns the signal back into sound.

MICROPHONES

Inside a microphone, there is a thin plate of metal or cardboard called a cone. The cone moves back and forth as sound waves hit it. In the moving coil microphone, a small coil of wire is fixed to the cone. This coil is near a magnet. The coil moves when the cone is moved by sound waves. When a wire moves in a magnetic field, an electric current flows in the wire. For this reason, an electric current is produced in the microphone's moving coil and passed to the amplifier, which magnifies the current. The current gets stronger or weaker as the sounds vary. A loudspeaker works in the opposite way to a microphone. The current from the amplifier is passed through a coil near an electromagnet, causing the coil to move. The coil is fixed to a cone which also moves causing the air to vibrate.

▲ A sound system is often made up of separate units. The record or cassette deck plays the record or tape, producing an electrical signal. The signal is increased in size, or amplified, by the amplifier unit.

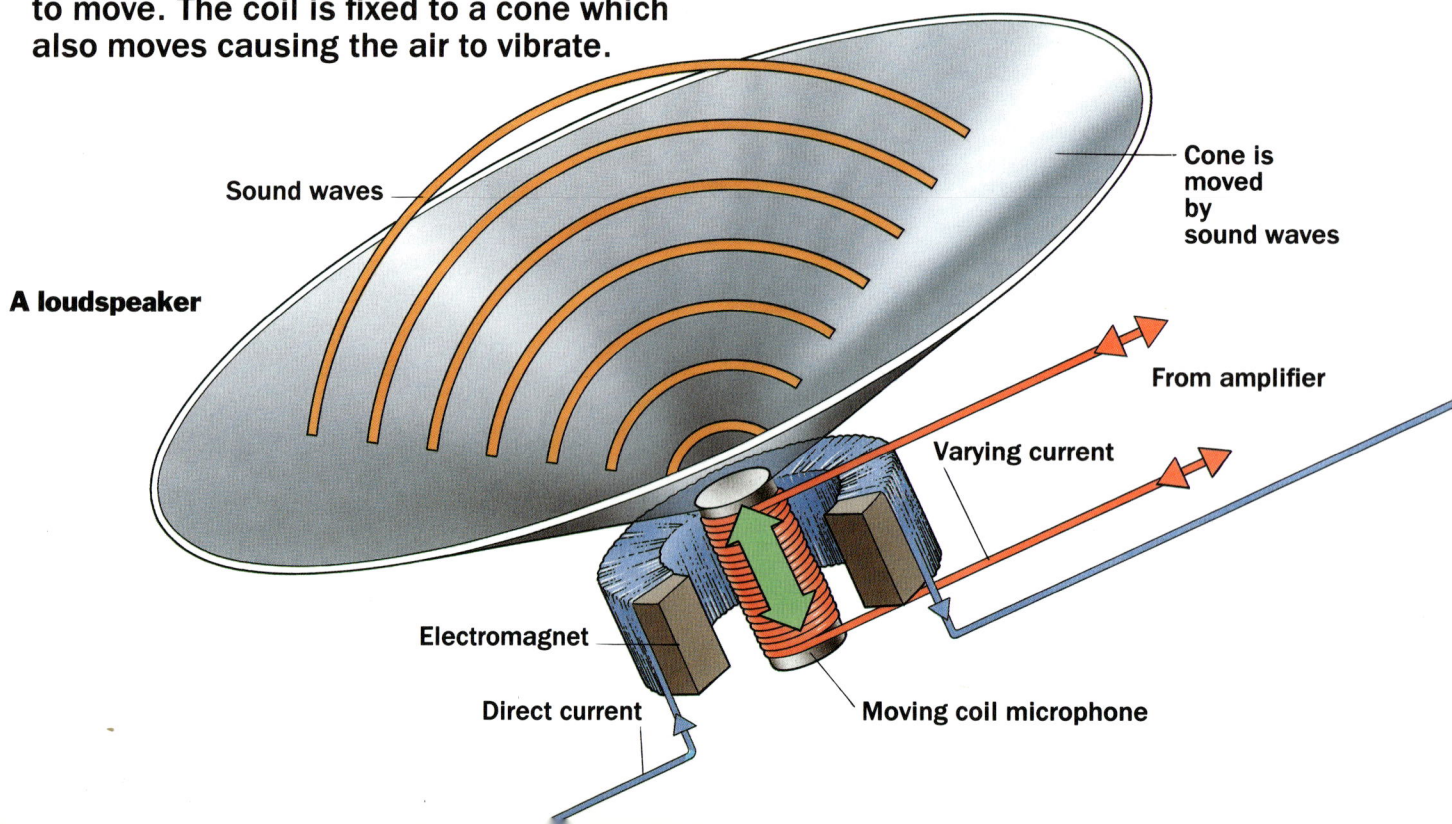

A loudspeaker

Sound waves

Cone is moved by sound waves

From amplifier

Varying current

Electromagnet

Direct current

Moving coil microphone

THE TAPE RECORDER

In a tape recorder, electrical signals from the amplifier are sent to the record/replay head. This contains coils of wire wrapped around cores, or rings, of metal which have a small gap cut in them. As the signals pass through the coils, a varying magnetic field is produced at the gap. The tape moves past the record head. This tape is made of a thin ribbon of plastic, covered with particles of magnetic material. As the tape moves past the head, the particles are magnetised into a pattern that represents the original sound. To play back the recording, the recorded tape is moved past the head. As it moves, the magnetic pattern on the tape produces a weak electric current in the head. This current is passed to the amplifier and loudspeaker.

▲ A tape recorder has an erase head as well as the record/play head. When recording, it is used to remove previous recording from the tape.

QUIZ

What happens if a magnet is dragged across a tape with sounds recorded on it? Will the recording on the tape be damaged? You can find the answer by experimenting with an *old* tape and a magnet.

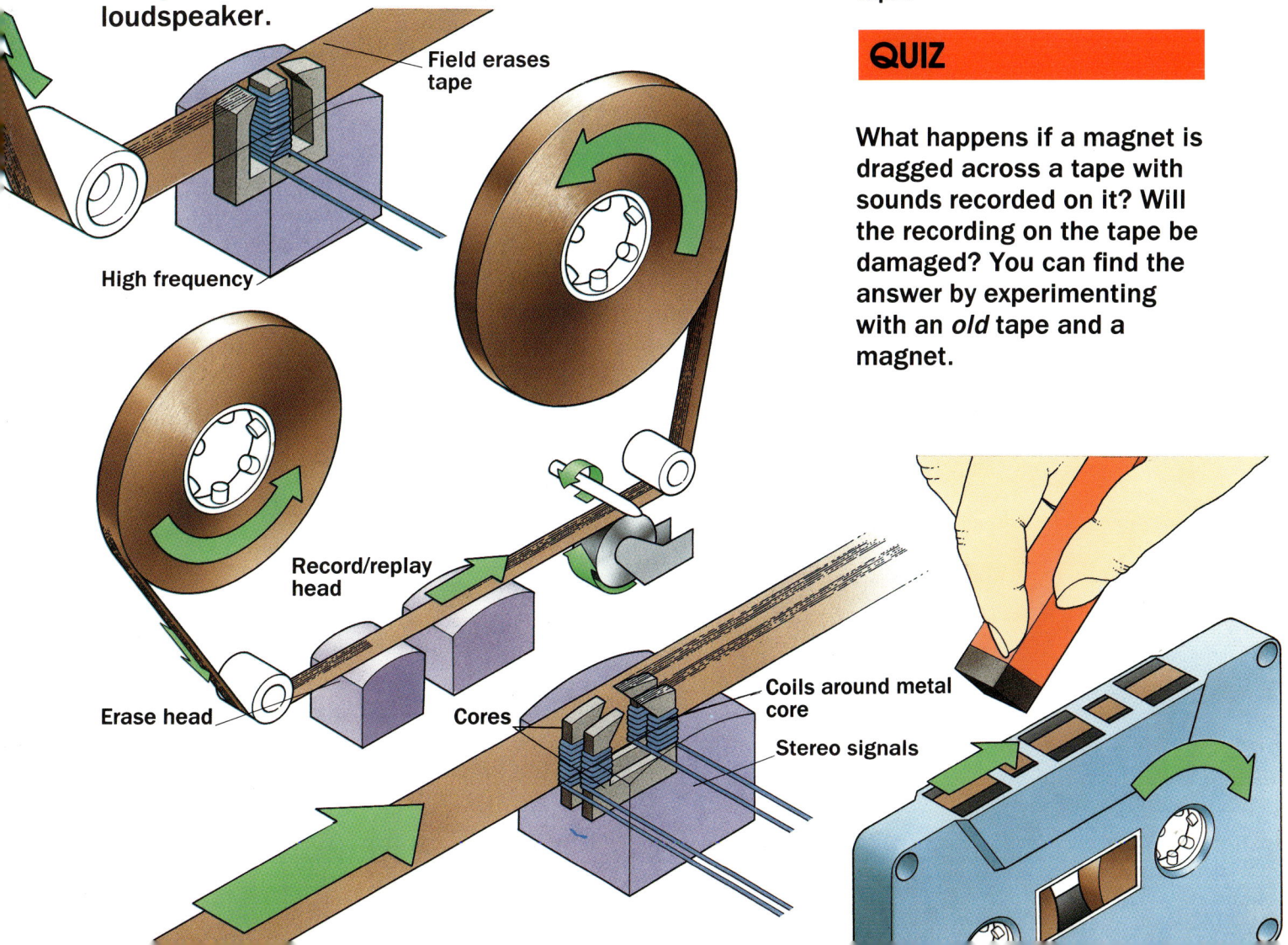

Field erases tape

High frequency

Record/replay head

Erase head

Cores

Coils around metal core

Stereo signals

Almost all our electricity supply is produced by dynamos containing magnets. In a dynamo, coils of wire rotate in a magnetic field to produce an electric current. Electric motors also contain magnets. But in a motor, a current passed through coils in a magnetic field causes the coils to rotate.

FARADAY'S EXPERIMENT

In 1831, an English scientist called Michael Faraday discovered how to use magnets to produce an electric current. He connected a coil of wire to a galvanometer, an instrument used to detect electric currents. When a bar magnet was pushed into the coil, the galvanometer needle moved slightly. Faraday realized that an electric current was produced as the magnet moved.

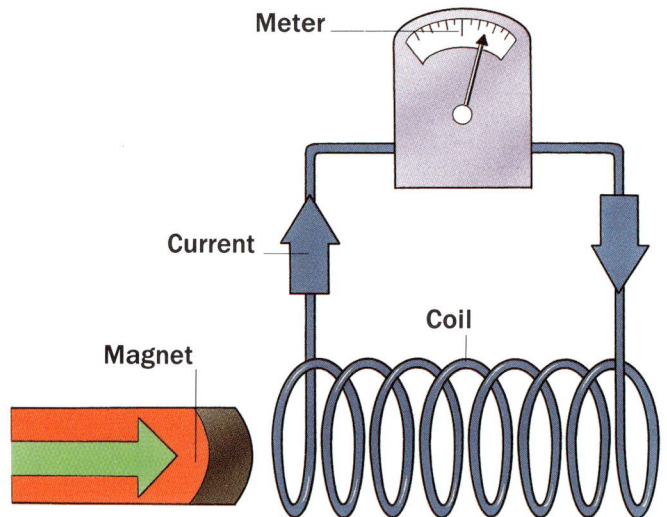

▲ The electric current flows in one direction as the magnet is moved into the coil. When the magnet is pulled out, the current moves in the other direction. When the magnet is still, no current is produced.

ELECTRIC CURRENT

Faraday put his discovery to good use by inventing the dynamo, a device for producing currents of electricity. The dynamo consisted of a coil of wire which was turned, or rotated, between the poles of a permanent magnet. The ends of the coil were connected to two half-circles of metal. Pieces of carbon, called brushes, pressed against the metal half-circles. As the coil turned, an electric current, called direct current, was produced.

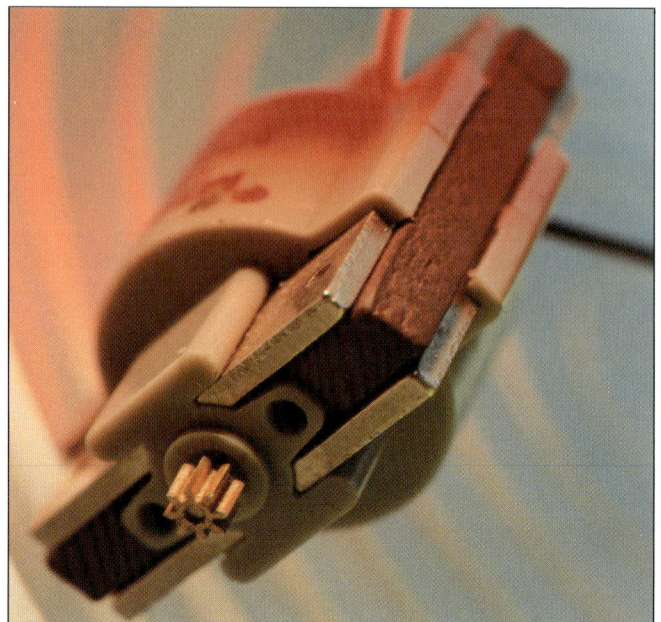

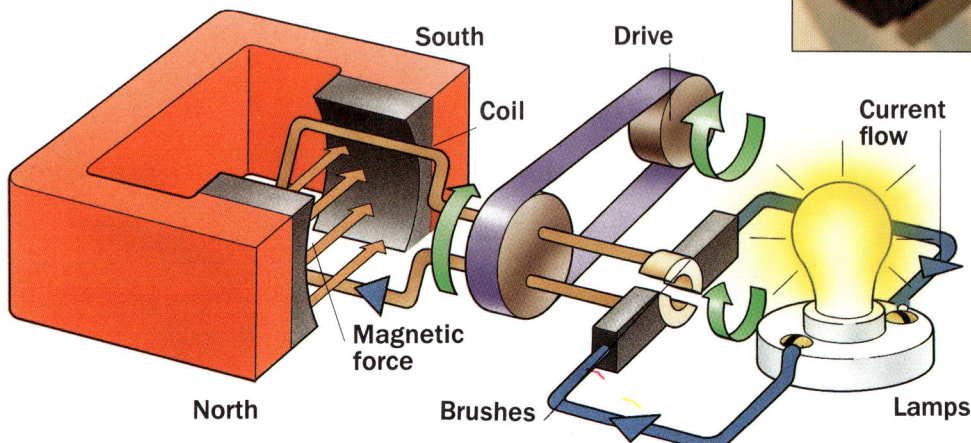

▲ A bicycle dynamo consists of a cylindrical permanent magnet which is turned by the bicycle wheel. The rotating magnet causes an electric current to flow in the coil of wire inside the dynamo. A wire carries the electric current to the bicycle lamp and the lamp lights up.

DYNAMOS IN USE

In an electric power station, huge dynamos, also called generators, are used to make electricity. These are often turned using steam power. Steam from boiling water is led through a pipe to a machine called a turbine. In hydroelectric power stations, water from a high dam is fed to the turbine. Inside the turbine, there are vanes like the vanes of a windmill. As the steam or water flows through the vanes, the turbine turns round. This turns an electromagnet inside a coil of wire. The effect is exactly the same as in a small dynamo, and electricity is produced in the coil.

▲ Some submarines have a generator powered by a nuclear reactor. A nuclear reactor has the advantage of being able to function under water for a long time without having to refuel.

◄ All power stations except hydroelectric ones use a fuel to produce steam which is then used to generate electricity. The fuel can be oil, gas, coal or nuclear fuel.

MOTORS

An electric motor is like a dynamo in reverse. It uses an electric current to provide a circular movement. Inside an electric motor there is a coil of wire. When an electric current is passed through the coil which is in a magnetic field, this coil turns around.

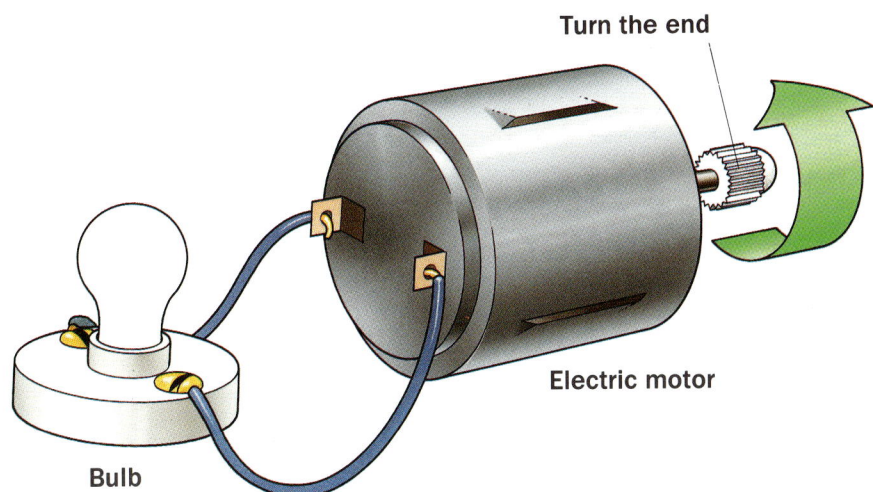

Turn the end

Electric motor

Bulb

Magnets have been studied over the ages, starting with the ancient Greeks in about 600BC and early Chinese scientists. Further important studies were made by William Gilbert in the time of Queen Elizabeth I. Today one of the main centres for the study of magnetism and electric current is CERN in Lucerne, Switzerland.

A huge industrial magnet.

Gilbert described how iron rods could be made into magnets by stroking them with lodestones. He also described how an iron rod became magnetised when pointed northwards and hammered. He discovered that the Earth behaves like a huge magnet whose poles do not match with true North and South. In fact he described the basic properties of magnets and his observations are still used by scientists. Gilbert was also the first person to use the word electricity derived from the Greek word "electron".

In 1820, a Danish scientist called Hans Oersted discovered a connection between electricity and magnetism. He noticed that a compass needle on his bench moved when electricity flowed through a nearby wire. Oersted's discovery was followed up by many other scientists, including the Englishman Michael Faraday. He made the first

Thomas Edison (1847-1931) invented the electric light bulb in 1879.

electric motor in 1821 and, in 1831, the first dynamo. In 1882, Thomas Edison, built the first electrical power station in New York. Within a few years, many large cities were lit by electricity, using the electric bulb invented by Edison in 1879. Scientists today are working on the use of magnets in the production of nuclear power.

Michael Faraday in 1842

Magnets in use at CERN

Amplifier
An electronic device which magnifies the strength of a signal, such as a radio signal.

Attract
To pull something with a force.

Compass
An instrument with a pivoted magnetic needle that always point northwards . It works because the needle lines itself parallel to the Earth's magnetic field.

Diaphragm
A thin metal or cardboard sheet that vibrates in a loudspeaker or microphone.

Domain
A very small region in a magnetic material that behaves like a tiny magnet.

Dynamo
A machine that uses the rotary motion of a coil in a magnetic field to produce an electric current.

Electric motor
A machine that uses an electric current to produce rotary motion of a coil in a magnetic field.

Electromagnet
A coil of wire with an iron bar inside it. It becomes a magnet when an electric current flows through the wire.

Ferrite
A type of magnetic material that can be formed into any shape and then baked hard in an oven.

Galvanometer
An instrument for measuring the strength of an electric current.

Induced magnetism
Magnetism caused in a magnetic material when a magnet is brought close.

Line of force
A line that shows the magnetic effect around a magnet. They can be seen by spreading fine iron filings around a magnet or bringing a compass up to it.

Lodestone
A type of rock which is a natural magnet. It contains the iron ore called magnetite.

Magnetic field
The space around a magnet where the magnetic effects can be felt.

Magnetic material
A material that is attracted by a magnet. Iron and steel, and a few other materials are magnetic.

Magnetic pole
The place on a magnet where the magnetic effect is strongest.

Non-magnetic material
A material that is not attracted by a magnet. Glass, wood and most metals except iron and steel are non-magnetic materials.

North magnetic pole
A place in northern Canada towards which a compass needle always points.

Repel
To push apart. Two similar magnetic poles repel each other.

Solenoid
A coil of wire that behaves like a magnet when an electric current passes through it.

Photographic Credits:
Cover and pages 15 and 18: J. Allan Cash Picture Library; pages 5, 6, 26 and back cover: Science Photo Library; page 9: Ford Motor Company; pages 10l, 27 and 28: Chapel Picture Library; pages 10 r and b, 13 and 23: Vanessa Bailey; pages 11 and 29: Paul Brierley; page 17: Robert Harding Library; page 29: Ministry of Defence; page 30tr: Frank Spooner Agency; page 30bl and br: Popperfoto.